Migration, Common Property Resources and Environmental Degradation

Migration, Common Property Resources and Environmental Degradation

Interlinkages in India's Arid and Semi-arid Regions

KANCHAN CHOPRA

S.C. GULATI

Sage Publications
New Delhi/Thousand Oaks/London

Copyright © Kanchan Chopra and S.C. Gulati, 2001

All rights reserved. No part of this book may be reproduced or utilised in any form or by any means, electronic or mechanical, including photocopying, recording or by any information storage or retrieval system, without permission in writing from the publisher.

First published in 2001 by

Sage Publications India Pvt. Ltd
M-32 Market, Greater Kailash, Part 1
New Delhi 110 048

Sage Publications Inc
2455 Teller Road
Thousand Oaks, California 91320

Sage Publications Ltd
6 Bonhill Street
London EC2A 4PU

Published by Tejeshwar Singh for Sage Publications India Pvt. Ltd., typeset by Deo Gratis Systems, Chennai, and printed at Chaman Enterprises, Delhi.

Library of Congress Cataloging-in-Publication Data
Chopra, Kanchan.
    Migration, common property resources and environmental degradation: interlinkages in India's arid and semi-arid regions / Kanchan Chopra, S.C. Gulati.
      p.   cm.
    Includes bibliographical references and index.
    1. Rural–urban migration—India. 2. Migration, Internal—India. 3. Environmental degradation—India. 4. Right of property—India. I. Gulati, S.C., 1945–II. Title.

HB2099.I4 C48   304.8'0954—dc21   2001   00-045672

ISBN: 0-7619-9501-3 (US-HB)   81-7036-982-7 (India-HB)

Sage Production Team: Anjana Malik, Sana Aiyar, M.S.V. Namboodiri, and Santosh Rawat

Contents

List of Tables, Maps and Figures	6
Preface	9
1. Rural–Urban Migration and Property Rights Structures	13
2. Common Property Resources in India: Magnitude and Distribution	22
3. Population Movements, Environmental Degradation and Property Rights: A District-level Analysis	44
4. Micro-level Initiatives in Semi-arid Zones: Emergence, Evolution and Impact	73
5. Non-governmental Initiatives in Natural Resource Management: A Profile of Study Villages	103
6. Participation, Common Property Institutions and Migration: An Econometric Exploration	120
7. Summary and Policy Recommendations	146
References	155
Index	161
About the Authors	164

List of Tables, Maps and Figures

TABLES

2.1	Identification of Common Property Resources	26
2.2	Components of Common Property Resources (000'HA) 1990–91	28
2.3	State-wise Magnitude of CPRs: 1990–91	30
2.4	Comparative Statistics on CPRs and Wastelands	32
2.5	Degraded Land and CPR Land (000'HA)	33
2.6	CPR Area in the Dry Tropical Regions	34
3.1	Characteristics of Agro-climatic Zones	47
3.2	Varimax Rotated Factor Structure	53
3.3	List of Selected Variables	57
3.4	3SLS Estimates of the Model	62
4.1	Phases in Evolution of NGO Activity: Udaipur District	79
4.2	Characteristics of Selected Projects	89
4.3	Nature of Association: Results from Village level Study	96
5.1	Socio-demographic Characteristics in the Study Villages	107
5.2	Health, Education and Community Infrastructure in the Six Villages	108
5.3	Access to Infrastructural Amenities in the Six Study Villages	109

5.4	Land Ownership and Use Patterns in the Study Villages	110
5.5	Drinking Water Resources	112
5.6	Nature of Irrigation from Seasonal Streams	112
5.7	Ownership Pattern of Sources of Irrigation	113
5.8	Groundwater Utilisation and its Characteristics	114
5.9	Cropping Pattern in the Study Villages	115
5.10	Livestock Population in the Study Villages	115
5.11	Quality and Utilisation of Forest Land	117
6.1	OLS Estimates of the Model with HMIG as the Response Variable	127
6.2	OLS Estimates of the Model with HCOM as the Response Variable	128
6.3	Effect on Participation in Common Land Resources (HPLI): Result of Logit Analysis	130
6.4	MCA Table of Adjusted Values of the Odds of Participation (W) and Probability of Participation (P) in Common Land Resources (HPLI)	131
6.5	Effect on Participation in Common Water Resources (HPWI): Results of Logit Analysis	132
6.6	MCA Table of Adjusted Values of the Odds of Participation (W) and Probability of Participation (P) in Common Water Resources (HPWI)	133
6.7	OLS Estimates of the Extent of Participation in Common Land Resources (HLDL)	135
6.8	OLS Estimates of the Extent of Participation in Common Water Resources (HLDW)	135
6.9	OLS Estimates of Stall Feeding (HSFI)	136
6.10	3SLS Estimates of Structural Parameters of Migrational and Participation Response Variables in the Models in the Text	137

APPENDIX TABLES

A3.1	Varimax Rotated Factor Structure for District's Natural and Migrational Growth Potential	67
A3.2	List of Selected Variables for Factorial Investigations	67

A3.3 Summary Statistics for Selected Variables for the
 Factorial Investigations 69
A3.4 List of Created Variables for the Simultaneous
 Structural System 70
A3.5 Summary Statistics for Created Variables for the
 Simultaneous Structural System 71
A3.6 Summary Statistics for the Selected Variables in the
 Simultaneous Structural System 71
A3.7 Reduced form Coefficients of the System 72

A4.1 Selected Indices for Udaipur and Rajasthan 98
A4.2 Areas of Activity of NGO's in Udaipur 99
A4.3 Support Linkages of UVM 100
A4.4 No. of Households in Contact with UVM 101

A6.1 Household Level Variables 141
A6.2 Summary Statistics for the Selected Variables 142
A6.3 Summary Statistics for the Selected Variables of the
 G.K. Vas Village 142
A6.4 Summary Statistics for the Selected Variables of the
 Dhar Village 143
A6.5 Summary Statistics for the Selected Variables of the
 Majjam Village 143
A6.6 Summary Statistics for the Selected Variables of the
 Bagduna Village 144
A6.7 Summary Statistics for the Selected Variables of the
 Bunadia Village 144
A6.8 Summary Statistics for the Selected Variables of the
 Patia Village 145

MAP

5.1 Udaipur District and Tehsils Gogunda and
 Girwa 106

FIGURE

4.1 NGO Intervention: Alternative Processes 77

Preface

The interlinkage between poverty and environmental degradation has been of interest to researchers in developing countries since the mid-eighties. Voices emanating from urban backgrounds have often claimed that poverty leads to environmental degradation. Degradation of the natural resource base in rural areas resulting in degradation-pushed migration to urban areas suggests the reverse direction of causation. It seems that degradation induced prevails in rural areas. What then is the nature of the relationship between poverty and environmental degradation? Some of us at the Institute of Economic Growth (IEG) felt that the issue was worthy of more in-depth study.

The idea received further impetus during the course of a short-term collaboration with the World Resources Institute (WRI), Washington, way back in 1993–94. The WRI had requested us to contribute a background paper on 'Population, environmental degradation and property rights' for their second India study. Given the time frame and the scope of the work, only a secondary data-based review study was called for and thus accomplished. The study again raised some interesting issues concerning factors determining the interlinkages between environmental degradation and poverty in the arid and semi-arid regions of the country. It was felt that the state of the commons plays an important role in determining the interlinkages between environmental degradation, poverty and distress out-migration in these regions. Furthermore, establishment or resurrection of properly-constituted common property rights through interventions in rural areas could hold the key to stemming the tide of both distress out-migration and environmental degradation.

The complex set of hypotheses could only be tested with detailed information and data inputs from a field-based survey. Intensive field work in Rajasthan was undertaken. During this period, our association with the functionaries of Ubeshwar Vikas Mandal (UVM) and Sewa Mandir enabled us to interact with a large number of village-based communities and to understand the dynamics of their behaviour vis-à-vis natural resources. The harsh realities faced by villagers and the attempted rural interventions by these organisations were also revealed to us. We recall, in particular, the detailed discussions on conceptual and practical aspects of development we had with Shri Kishore Saint, who had initiated Ubeshwar Vikas Mandal, which was instrumental in leading to the upliftment of several tribal villages in Rajasthan. We owe special gratitude to Shri Kishore Saint and many others working in his organisation with whom we interacted and which facilitated the enrichment of the present study.

The major point of departure of this study is an attempt to use econometric techniques to view institutional change in rural areas and determine its impact on environmental upgradation, socio-economic conditions and distress out-migration from rural tracts. Simultaneously, organisational evolution of the outside institutions has also been studied. It is hoped that the study will provide some insights into the complex linkages between people and the environment from which they derive their livelihoods.

We are indebted to many people for their academic inputs. A number of our younger colleagues at IEG have contributed to the volume. We owe special thanks to Dr Suresh Sharma for his diligent coordination of field work and analysis of statistical data. Ms Seema Bathla and Ms Preeti Kapuria contributed with their enthusiastic assistance in literature search, data analysis and compilation. Professor Gopal Kadekodi was generous with his time in providing useful suggestions at all stages of the study. Parts of the study were presented at a staff seminar at IEG and we are grateful to the participants for their valuable comments.

Parts of the present volume have already been published as journal articles, in *Environmental and Resource Economics, Environment and Development Economics* and *Demography India*. We are grateful to the referees of the journals for comments that helped improve the contents. A part of the volume was presented at a seminar organised by the Centre for Science and Environment, New Delhi and subsequently published in a book edited by Anil Agarwal entitled *The Challenge of the Balance*.

We also wish to place on record our special gratitude to Professor Pravin Visaria, Director, IEG for his constant support and encouragement in both academic and administrative matters. But for his help the volume would not have taken its present shape. Needless to say, we own responsibility for the deficiencies that still remain.

KANCHAN CHOPRA
S.C. GULATI

Chapter 1
Rural–Urban Migration and Property Rights Structures

1.1 Poverty and Environmental Degradation: The Issue and the Context

The poverty–environmental quality debate has now a considerably long lineage. Theoretical literature and empirical evidence often contend that poverty results in environmental degradation, in particular, of the kind related to depletion and degradation of natural resource endowments. Furthermore, excessive population growth in such a situation compounds the adverse impact of poverty on environmental degradation. Such a contention derives support from analytical frameworks based on a modified 'tragedy of the commons' stand. The argument often runs thus: higher levels of poverty and population growth constitute increased pressure on natural resources since such resources often cannot be excluded from use by all groups. Increased pressure of demand, therefore, results in progressive deterioration of the natural resources. Further, rates of discount for future are high at low levels of current income, satisfaction of present demand becomes the first priority and high levels of demand which far exceed the rate of regeneration are generated. Consequently, depletion of the environment is the expected outcome.

At the macro level, the environmental Kuznets curve hypothesis postulates that higher levels of consumption as exemplified by higher national products, beyond a point, are accompanied with lower levels of environmental degradation. Even though the evidence is mixed, the argument seems to be: pursue development, and the environment will take care of itself. Looked at from another viewpoint, a question that may well be asked is: do all developing countries have necessarily to pass through the earlier part of the Kuznets process as well, with rising incomes resulting in more environmental degradation? This volume argues that this is not so. Latecomers on the development scene can learn in a number of ways. A kind of 'leap-frogging' is possible. They can adopt greener technologies, in particular when globalisation and information technology make access to them easy. More importantly, they can evolve their own institutional and technological options. As reiterated by the large and growing literature on the many aspects of the links between poverty and environmental degradation, it is hazardous to accept highly simplified constructs such as the environmental Kuznets curve.[2] A large variety of technological options and institutional structures evolve and coexist in developing economies. While some of these structures permit open access to environmental resources and hence their degradation, others are seen to play a useful role in preventing environmental degradation. Communities, often with outside non-governmental and/or governmental support, are seen to get motivated for collective action towards preservation of environmental resources which plays a crucial role in supporting livelihoods and consumption levels. One of the outcomes of such experiments is an increase in the capacity of the environment to support larger populations. In other words, the 'carrying capacity' of the land increases. The implication is, of course, that a change in the manner in which people relate to resources prevents them from being degraded. In other words, the link between population and environmental degradation is not a simple arithmetic one but is mediated by the institutional framework within which it takes place.

In this context, an institutional framework is a codified set of rules, which, by convention or by law, mediates the nature of the relationship between people and resources. It creates the configuration within which economic transactions take place in the short run and resource management takes place in the medium and longer runs. Specific tasks that institutions for natural resource management need to address are:

(1) Finding a method of rationing scarce resources in situations where the nature of the resource pre-empts the existence of a market.

(2) Building on a system of inter-temporal allocation that overrides possible preferences of individuals for the present.
(3) Ensuring sustainable use of the resources.

The form of such institutions may need to change with time as population increases, demands multiply and outside forces impinge on rural economies. This calls for institutional innovation. Such innovation replaces existing structures of social interaction with newer but more efficient ones. It is a dynamic process in which the interface of the society with the rest of the world plays an important role. In rural India of the eighties and nineties, for instance, the village community has witnessed such an interface. Consequently it has created and strengthened its contacts with the city both through population movements and through the introduction of new kinds of goods and services in rural areas. Increasing contact with village society has also meant that people from cities have been exposed to the changes taking place in the countryside, both those of a beneficial and a not-so beneficial nature. One outcome of such two-way contact has been the attempt by a few urban-based individuals to understand and participate in the functioning of village institutions, among others, in the area of natural resource management.

It is perhaps on account of this that a large array of non-governmental interventions in the area of natural resource management has its origins in urban India. Such intervention, even when it is the outcome of participatory action research, can be termed induced institutional innovation. It stands in contrast to the slowly evolving institutions of rural society. Such induced innovatory experiments have, however, an important role to play. It can be postulated, for instance, that such institutional changes have an impact on productivity and hence, on the links between population and environmental degradation through the creation of well-specified property rights and methods of their implementation. An analysis of this role is significant, in particular, in the context of migration and the questions being asked about the links between population and environmental degradation.

The present volume is an attempt in this direction. The rest of this chapter focuses on the analytical dimensions of alternative property-rights structures in natural resources, especially in land and water, and a possible hypothesis linking them with rural–urban distress migration. The second chapter sets out the possible magnitude of the problem in the context of the country as a whole, and of the arid and semi-arid regions in particular. The chapters that follow are an in-depth exploration of the links between migration and the management of common property. This is done first from the macro angle of the arid and semi-arid regions of India and then in the more micro context of the region, particularly in Udaipur district of Rajasthan. The methodology followed uses econometric techniques to capture the relationships between different variables. Successively desegregated levels of analysis are employed to look at the same hypotheses and test them in different ways. This is considered important because the use of econometric techniques in this area is still comparatively new. To supplement such analysis the fourth chapter presents an account of processes underlying the evolution and working of two organisations representing different paradigms with respect to rural development in India. In addition, this chapter attempts to capture the inter-relationships between indices of migration, environmental improvement and related variables derived from studies of experiments in different semi-arid regions of India. The last chapter provides pointers towards policy implications of the study.

1.2 Property Rights Structures: A Classification

The nature of rights in property constitutes a significant part of the institutional structure of any community. It defines how people relate to resources and use them. Analysts refer to a continuum of property rights, with the dominant control of ownership and user rights over the resource changing from point to point within the continuum. Four important kinds of property rights arrangements in existence within this continuum are: private, common, state, and open access.[3] Each of these forms defines, in effect, the bounds of control of the major right holder. No right in property can ever be absolute and undeterred. Even the most rigid private property institution is restricted by the dictates of what constitutes legal use. Further, limits to the exercise of private property rights are often set by the state in view of the emerging significance of environmental or amenity values in adjacent property. In a similar manner, an extension of the frontier of private property has resulted in a reduction of the realm of common property. The inefficacy of state control as the dominant form of property ownership has led to the emergence of community forms of control. In brief, if the players outside the bounds of any form of property rights structure find that a change in it is beneficial to them and if they are in a position to alter the structure of control, they shall attempt to do so. Whether or not they are successful shall depend on their capability to meet the transaction cost of the change.

In such a scenario, the emergence of common property institutions as more efficient forms of social organisation may have a number of causal factors. Some emerge because of the existence of environmental resources as commonly consumed commodities. It has been found, for instance, that the presence of exploitable groundwater (a resource which a number of private land owners have access to) has often resulted in a shift towards common property rights in water. Such an impact of private land ownership on groundwater levels and it's overexploitation in the semi-arid region around Los Angeles is noteworthy.[4] The agreements to curtail water withdrawals were arrived at voluntarily, implying an institutional transformation from private towards common property rights.

The existence of an ecosystem within which all economic activity takes place often results in inter-relationships commonly referred to as externalities. State intervention to extend the domain of its rights in the presence of externalities constitutes the textbook case of a redefinition of a property rights frontier. Much less understood, but perhaps of equal importance, is the traditional definition and redefinition of such frontiers implicit in the relationships between herders and sedentary agriculturists in large parts of the arid and semi-arid regions of the world. The agriculturists, recognising the contribution of animal herds to rejuvenation of soil fertility, provide rights of passage and temporary user rights in their land to herders.[5] Another aspect of the same ecological perspective is the reiteration that best land use is an eco-system specific concept.[6] Also, with the value attached to biodiversity, preservation of diverse ecosystems has an option and an existence value and this objective creates the need for diverse property rights structures as well.

The existence of a minimum economic scale factor may sometimes mean the superiority of a common property scheme of management. Small fragments of submarginal land often remain uncultivated under private property regimes. A pooling together with the creation of common infrastructural assets, once suggested and implemented as a possible option, results in an increase in land productivity.

It can be postulated, therefore, that a rich diversity of property rights structures is feasible and is found to exist on the ground. The effect that they have on the links between population and environmental degradation needs to be evaluated carefully. Such an analysis is significant, in particular, in the context of the questions being asked about the efficiency of population policy.[7] In the developing country context the necessity for a well articulated policy to attempt decreased rates of population growth is paramount. It is our contention that an understanding of the role of alternative property rights structures and their links with natural resource potential is an important input in the formulation of such a policy.

1.3 Rural–Urban Migration: A Hypothesis

The literature on internal, in particular rural–urban, migration in developing countries has viewed the problem from a number of different angles. In the early literature, rural–urban migration was considered desirable as it provided labour for the growth of the industrial sector. Over time, it was found that in most countries, migration far exceeded the rate of employment creation. It was, in part, this trend that led studies to focus on the micro-economic foundations of the behaviour of individuals in the decision to migrate. The Todaro hypothesis, which was a major watershed in the work on migration, postulated that migration occurred in response to (*a*) rural–urban differences in expected rather than actual earnings and (*b*) the probability of getting work.

Simultaneously, social and cultural factors entering the migration decision did receive some attention. However, the overwhelming conclusion of most empirical studies was that people migrate for economic reasons. In the case of India, for instance, Greenwood's study found that migration was related positively and significantly to wage at the destination point, and negatively and significantly to wage at the point of origin.[8]

In the above context, some studies examined the genesis of the expected income differentials between rural and urban areas. The effect of trade unions and other institutional factors on this wage differential was recognised. The effect of migration on the differences between source and destination areas also attracted attention. Considering the impact of an increasing population on the urban environment, it was recognised that rural–urban migration was not necessarily desirable.

It was found in some studies, for instance, that internal migration may affect adversely the welfare of the source areas[9] while contributing little to increased social welfare in urban areas.

Some factors affecting micro-economic behaviour of migrants, however, have received little attention. One of these is changing institutions in the rural sector which influence migrant behaviour primarily through their effect on the rural–urban income differential. Incomes in the rural economy are typically the sum of those obtained from private property resources and those received from common property resources. A strengthening of common property rights institutions is expected to increase the probability of obtaining a sustained level of income from them, thereby tending to reduce the rural–urban income differential and decreasing the propensity to migrate. In other words, the increased capacity of resources to sustain populations becomes a disincentive to migrate. It is postulated in this volume that this may be true, in particular, in arid and semi-arid regions where common property resources constitute a large part of the consumption base of the poor[10] and where distress migration resulting from environmental degradation comprises a significant part of total migration.

1.4 Is there a Carrying Capacity Concept Inherent in this Hypothesis?

The concept of carrying capacity has been the theme of a number of studies, both ecological and economic.[11] A study of alternative approaches to the estimation of the earth's carrying capacity, starting from the late seventeenth century and going up to the latter half of the twentieth century reveals that factors acting as constraints on it are:

(1) Land, water: both quality and quantity.
(2) Use of photosynthesis and energy.
(3) Nature of and changes in technology.
(4) Social institutions.
(5) Culturally-determined definitions of what constitutes a resource, and, finally and perhaps most importantly,
(6) The level of living at which the population is to be supported.

It is our considered opinion that the extent to which each of the factors mentioned above could change over time and space makes almost all estimates of the earth's carrying capacity suspect. It even brings into question the meaningfulness of the enterprise. Demographers, in particular, are very cautious when it comes to carrying capacity estimates as they believe that the interactions involved in determining world populations themselves are far too complex.

This study does not attempt to say anything on total carrying capacity, even within the context of the region of the study. It only analyses the role of property rights institutions on the production of incremental resources and hence, the capacity to support additional populations, the latter taking the form of a decrease in out-migration. A large number of other factors affecting the carrying capacity of the region are taken to be constant. Examples of these are consumption levels, technology and cultural perceptions of what constitutes a resource. The focus is on the changes that property rights alterations can bring about in a situation of environmental degradation. Any conclusions with respect to the carrying capacity are secondary.

ENDNOTES

1. The World Development Report (1992) was among the first to popularise the existence of such a relationship. The evidence on its existence is mixed with concentration of some pollutants following the inverted U-shape, others increasing exponentially and still others following a kind of jagged N-shape. See Shafik and Banddopadhyay (1992) and Seldon and Song (1994).
2. Bromley (1991) has put together evidence from a number of countries across the developing world to illustrate how intentional policies of governments in need of foreign exchange, well-intended but mis-specified policies and broad agricultural sector policies cause problems for land use and natural resources. See also Repetto and Gillis et al. (1988), Repetto and Holmes (1983). For the impact of the market on natural resource use, see Gadgil (1992). For an analysis of the role of property rights in the linkages between poverty and degradation, see, among others, Chopra and Rao (1992, 1997).
3. See Bromley (1991) and Ciriacy-Wanthrop and Bishop (1975) for the definitions and specifications of this continuum.
4. See Ostrom (1990) for an in-depth analysis of institutional change with accompanying changes in property rights.
5. See the work of Wade (1988) on south India. Also Cincotti and Pangare (1993) on pastoralists in western India.
6. It can however be argued that this changes land use and can be reflected in a private property situation, which constituted the basis of an experiment in Bihar. See Chopra and Kadekodi (1999).

7. See among others Srinivasan (1993) in the wider context of India's population policy.
8. See Greenwood (1971a, 1971b).
9. See, for example, Lipton (1976) and Connell et al. (1975).
10. For an empirical study of the contribution of common property resources to the consumption base of the poor in arid and semi-arid regions of India, see Jodha (1986).
11. See Cohen (1995) for a verbal definition of carrying capacity; Appendix 4 in the book gives 26 such definitions of carrying capacity.

Chapter 2

Common Property Resources in India: Magnitude and Distribution

2.1 Introduction

The previous chapter hypothesised that the existence of well-defined property rights in rural land and related resources impacts people's expectations with respect to income accruals from them, both in the present and the future. The question however arises: what is the magnitude of land on which different levels of unspecified or unimplementable rights exist and which can therefore, be viewed as an area where correction in property rights arrangements is conceivable? This chapter attempts to answer this question in the Indian context. In the first two sections, property rights arrangements are classified and defined with respect to existing land use categories. The subsequent sections examine existing data on land use classifications and set up a methodology for estimating common property land resources at the state level. The estimates are then compared with alternative estimates of wastelands to study the extent of overlap, if any.

2.2 Property Rights Arrangements

Common property resources (CPRs) are often viewed in general parlance as a category on which ambiguous rights exist. This perception is at variance with the perception in the literature on property rights, which conceptualises common property as 'private property for a group'[1] with organisational rules circumscribing the nature of rights and responsibilities existing within the group with respect to them.

The difference in perception between the popular and the documented views is mainly due to the varying degrees of open access that now exist on common property as a consequence of the breakdown of the organisational systems associated with it. In actual practice, varying degrees of access always exist. A distinction, for instance, could be made between ownership rights and user rights. In a functional sense at the village level, the rights and the conditions that go with it are clear. Multiple uses and inter-related rights are the order of the day as any perceptive observer of the rural scene knows. Further, sets of resources are sometimes characterised by complementarity in use, the linkages between these uses giving rise to common property rights regimes of differing kinds. Examples are easily found in rural societies in the context of water bodies accessed, for different purposes or by different groups of communities. Land situated in different parts of a watershed or a tank is used by different sets of right-holders at different times of the agricultural year. In parts of Tamil Nadu, for instance, landowners in the ayacut of a tank have prior right to the water for irrigation over landowners on the tankfore, even though the tank is treated as community property.[2] It is common for nomadic communities to possess sheep-penning rights on private farmland in parts of Karnataka, Gujarat and other parts of semi-arid India.[3] Similarly, grazing rights on private land are accorded to pastoral communities after the harvesting of the monsoon crop. Institutions formalising such combinations of common and private property rights continue to thrive as long as it is to the mutual advantage of the stakeholders. In other words, user rights may exist for certain purposes and at certain times. A complex mosaic of property rights regimes is 'therefore' found to exist in different parts of the country.

It may be useful to point out that a large number of such institutional arrangements are the consequence of a continuous interaction between vested interest groups at local levels and it is not correct to surmise that equity plays an important role in their functioning. 'Mutual advantage' is often conditioned by the existing power structures.

Further, changing technology and increasing pressure on land are bound to destabilise these institutions, reflecting as they do local nuances. This process of destabilisation results in ambiguity with respect to the structure of rights and duties, reinforcing the understanding popularly held that common property resources are indeed open access resources.

2.3 Existing Land Use Classifications

As against the above picture of nuances in gradation of property rights regimes, the policy maker who is examining the scope for possible creation of interventions based on collective action aims at estimating 'common property resources' at the state or the national level. The focus here is on determining magnitudes of land area where such interventions can be meaningfully initiated within the context of existing land use. Property rights classifications need to be examined in the context of existing classifications of land use to be able to do this. Such an exercise is significant in a macro-policy perspective even though some assumptions with respect to coverage are inevitable in such an exercise.

A number of alternative classifications of the land area of India are available. First, there exists the nine-fold classification of land use as reported in agricultural statistics (ALUS).[4] This can delineate use categories but not ownership categories that can only be inferred indirectly. Ownership with respect to agricultural land is specified additionally in the Agricultural Censuses (AC), as a part of which data is collected once every five years. Here, the main distinction focused upon is between ownership holdings and operational holdings.

Further, forest land—one of the categories in the nine-fold classification—is distinguished between on the basis of categories of forests such as reserved, protected and unclassed forests, and these have connotations with regard to the nature of people's rights existing on them.[5] Legal ownership of 95.8 per cent of the forest area is vested in the state. Only 2.5 per cent of the forest area is with corporate bodies, defined as 'municipal and other corporate bodies, village panchayats etc'. Rights of access to parts of the state-owned forest have, however, existed for local communities. State-owned forests can be reserved, protected or unclassed, depending on the category of forest cover. Though reserve forests have always been treated as inaccessible, protected and unclassed forests are partly accessible. As far back as in 1907, the Imperial Gazetteer recorded that the unclassed or public forest lands are those given over with even fewer restrictions for the use of the public.[6] It further maintained that protected forests may be either in a state of transition to reserves, or intended to remain permanently in that class. In the latter case, more beneficial exercise of rights by local communities was allowed. It can, therefore, be concluded that access of local communities to protected forests would be inversely related to the magnitude of their conversion to reserve forests. The Government of India Gazetteer of 1975 also holds that the local people have virtually unrestricted rights of felling trees and grazing livestock in protected forests.[7] On the basis of these pieces of indirect evidence, it can be concluded that whereas no access to reserve forests has been granted either by law or by use,[8] local communities have had access to protected forests both by law and, more significantly, by convention.

Land may also sometimes be categorised by the physical status of the land as observed, in particular, with reference to different kinds of degradation. Wasteland, for instance, is defined as 'degraded land that can be brought under vegetative cover with reasonable effort and which is currently under-utilised land and land which is deteriorating due to lack of appropriate water and soil management or on account of natural causes'. Early attempts in estimating wasteland using such a category made primarily by the National Wasteland Development Board (NWDB), were based on a reclassification of land use data.[9]

Remote sensing techniques (NRSA) provide an alternative classification of land use/land cover based on 22 categories of land use. Seven of these categories comprise non-forest wasteland and two can be classified as wasteland falling within forests. The NRSA has two sets of estimates of wastelands in India using data based on these techniques.[10] The first uses Lands at data derived from a 1:1 million scale of mapping. The second uses LISS-1 and LISS-2 data with a 1:250,000 mapping. These two sets give differing estimates of wastelands. The second estimate puts wastelands at 75.53 million hectares, the first at 53.3 million hectares. Both estimates yield a much lower figure for wastelands than the NWDB data.

Apart from the differences in estimates arising out of the use of different methodologies, none of these classifications is based exclusively on property rights which should, in effect, distinguish between private, communal, open access and state ownership. In this chapter, an attempt is made to develop a methodology to estimate the magnitude of one such property rights determined category: common property resources (CPR) in land in India. We shall estimate CPRs in land for 1990–91 as a starting point.[11]

2.4 A Methodology for Estimating Common Property Resources and Some Estimates

As stated in section 2.2, rights to common property resources are a matter of observation and record, based on degree of access arising out of both ownership and use. Methodologies based on secondary data, where classifications of the kind listed in section 2.3 exist, cannot capture all the ramifications of this access. The attempt to determine broad orders of magnitude will be based, therefore, on assumptions with respect to both ownership and user rights dimensions, and may involve over-estimation or under-estimation in specific categories. The attempt is aimed at determining ranges within which the estimates fall, with a view to providing directions for policy.

Estimates are made for 16 major states.[12] Table 2.1 gives the land use classification as available in the official statistics in India (ALUS) and the assumptions made by us regarding levels and sanctions for access as common property. The first column of Table 2.1 lists the eight categories into which official land use statistics[13] classify geographical land. Net sown area (including area under miscellaneous

TABLE 2.1
Identification of Common Property Resources

Classification	Included in CPR	Source of Sanction for Land Access (as assumed in the estimation)
Net Sown Area	No	On uncultivated owned land: limited user rights
Current Fallow	No	On uncultivated owned land: limited user rights
Fallow Other Than	Yes	User rights by convention current
Cultivable Waste	Yes, partial	User rights by convention
Pastures and Other Grazing Land	Yes	User rights by law
Barren and Uncultivable Land	May be included	No access
Area Put to Non-Agricultural Use	No	No access
Forest Area		
1. Reserved	No	No access
2. Protected	Partial	Partial user rights
3. Unclassed	Yes	User rights by law

tree crops) and current fallow constitute together a private property resource to which non-owners do not generally have access. However, partial access has been found to exist to owned land which may remain uncultivated due to some exigency. This could be absence of capital investment or the sheer fact that the owner does not consider it worthwhile to invest in marginal or submarginal land. For determining the magnitude of such land, the following methodology is adopted.

Data on owned land obtained from the Agricultural Census (AC) (1985–86) is compared to that on net area sown and current fallow obtained from official statistics (ALUS) is made.[14] Since at the state level total land leased in is approximately equal to land leased out, it is assumed that area owned and operated are equal for each state. Wherever area owned obtained from the Agricultural Census exceeds the sum of net area sown and current fallow as obtained from the land use statistics, it is assumed that rights of common access exist on this surplus land (column two of Table 2.2). This may or may not be marginal land. In other words, private land to which common access may exist (PLCPR) is equal to:

PLCPR = TOTAL OWNED AREA (Obtained From AC) − (NET SOWN AREA + CURRENT FALLOWS) (Obtained From ALUS) (1)

Such a comparison of the two data sources reveals that in 1991, limited common access to uncultivated private land existed in the seven states of Andhra Pradesh, Bihar, Himachal Pradesh, Karnataka, Madhya Pradesh, Maharashtra and Rajasthan and to an almost negligible extent in Tamil Nadu. A comparison with earlier estimates for 1980–81 shows that magnitudes of private land to which common access could have been permissible seem to have decreased significantly in all states except Tamil Nadu and Karnataka.[15]

Columns three, four and five of Table 2.2 list the area of fallows other than current, cultivable wastes (including pastures and other grazing lands) for 1990–91. Partial or complete access is permitted to these areas either by law or by convention. These are, therefore, included in the estimation of common property resources.[16]

The next category of land to which common property rights may exist is land under forests divided into reserved, protected and unclassed forests. In our estimates, protected and unclassed forests are treated as forming a part of common property resources, keeping in mind that this may yield an over-estimate of land to which common property may exist.[17]

It is therefore, the subset of total forest area minus reserve forests to which common property rights are assumed to exist. State-wise total forest area is taken from NRSA estimates. Reserve forest, being a legal classification, has to be obtained from land use data. The total common property resources in land are thus defined as the sum of:

1. that part of land which, though officially classified as privately-owned, allows partial common access since it is not sown on,

TABLE 2.2
Components of Common Property Resources (000'HA) 1990–91

State	PLCPR	PROT& UNCL	PPG	CWL	FL	CPR	Forests
Andhra Pradesh	1624	1365	843	780	1377	5989	27507
Bihar	1353	2417	126	372	999	5267	17387
Gujarat	0	562	849	1920	60	3269	19602
Haryana	0	146	23	21	–	19	4421
Himachal Pradesh	343	3569	1136	125	15	5188	5567
Jammu & Kashmir	7	0	127	138	6	278	22223
Karnataka	202	1004	1098	446	457	3207	19179
Kerala	0	207	2	95	27	331	3886
Madhya Pradesh	1307	7444	2734	1529	826	13890	44345
Maharashtra	2396	2113	1519	1028	983	8039	30769
Orissa	0	3345	726	597	214	4882	15571
Punjab	0	2126	10	35	28	2119	5036
Rajasthan	2291	280	1912	5567	1028	11977	34224
Tamil Nadu	929	386	124	290	1044	2773	13006
Uttar Pradesh	0	1535	303	1034	884	3756	29441
West Bengal	0	483	7	106	51	647	8875

Sources: Agricultural Statistics of India, Agriculture Census, Forest Statistics, The State of Forest Report, The State of India's Environment.

Abbreviations Used:
PLCPR : Private Land to which common access may exist
PROT&
  UNCL: Protected and Unclassed Forest Land
PPG   : Other Uncultivated Lands like Permanent Pastures and Grazing Land excluding Current Fallows
CWL   : Culturable Waste Lands
FL   : Fallow Land other than Current Fallows
CPR   : Common Property Resources
TGA   : Trans-Geographical Area

2. cultivable wastes and fallows other than current,
3. common pastures and grazing land, and
4. protected and unclassed forests.

Common property resource area, so defined, comes to between 4 and 32 per cent of the total geographical area of the different states in the early nineties if the outliers (Himachal Pradesh and Rajasthan) are left out.

A close examination of CPR estimates suggests division of the states into three groups:

1. States where the CPR area is low, being less than or around 10 per cent of the geographical area in both years. Punjab and Haryana fall in this category. These two states are at an advanced level of agricultural development and are characterised by a large percentage of land under private ownership. Correspondingly, CPR area per capita is low.
2. States where the CPR area falls in the range of around 10 to 30 per cent. A number of states such as Andhra Pradesh, Bihar, Gujarat, Karnataka, Kerala, Madhya Pradesh, Maharashtra, Orissa, Tamil Nadu and Uttar Pradesh fall in this group.
3. The outliers constitute a separate category. Rajasthan has a CPR area of 35 per cent, which seems to be an over-estimation.[18] Himachal Pradesh and Jammu and Kashmir, on account of being hilly states, show varying characteristics. This is because of large areas of protected forests in Himachal Pradesh which makes the area under CPRs unduly high and similar large areas in the category of reserve forests in Jammu and Kashmir which decreases CPR area to an unusually low level.

Non-forest CPR land is shown separately in Table 2.3 in order to eliminate the effect of such classification of forest area on the estimates. This estimate also has the benefit of showing the extent of CPR access to land under the jurisdiction of private persons or local bodies.

Total CPR land in the 16 states is 70.042 million hectares. Of this 44.983 million hectares or about 64.23 per cent is non-forest land. As stated earlier, estimates have not been made for the north-eastern states in which there is reason to believe land records are faulty. Available estimates indicate that if these states are also taken into account, total CPR area increases to 74.573 million hectares. Further, CPR area varies from 25 to 52 per cent of geographical area in these states.[19]

Changes over time in the magnitude of CPR land both as percentages of the geographical area and in per capita terms can be estimated. It is found that in a majority of the states, there has occurred a decrease in the land to which CPR rights exist. Per capita CPR land has also gone down. These decreases are more pronounced in the arid and semi-arid states of Madhya Pradesh, Maharashtra, Gujarat, Karnataka, and Rajasthan.

It is found that both levels of CPR area in different states and changes taking place over time have exhibited interesting patterns. River basins, where crop production on private land is a profitable activity, have a low percentage whereas high rainfall mountains and sub-mountainous regions have a high percentage. Arid and semi-arid

TABLE 2.3
State-wise Magnitude of CPRs: 1990–91

State	Total CPR (000' HA)	Non-forest CPR (000' HA)	CPR/GA (HA)	CPR per capita (HA)	NF-CPR/GA (HA)
Andhra Pradesh	5989	4624	0.22	.09	0.16
Bihar	5267	2850	0.30	.06	0.16
Gujarat	3269	2707	0.17	.08	0.14
Haryana	190	44	0.04	.01	.009
Himachal Pradesh	5188	1619	0.93	1.00	0.29
Jammu & Kashmir	278	278	0.012	.06	0
Karnataka	3207	2203	0.17	.07	0.11
Kerala	331	207	0.08	.01	0.05
Madhya Pradesh	13890	6446	0.32	0.21	0.15
Maharashtra	8039	5926	0.26	0.10	0.19
Orissa	4882	1537	0.31	0.15	0.09
Punjab	359	73	0.07	0.01	0.014
Rajasthan	11977	11697	0.35	0.27	0.34
Tamil Nadu	2773	2387	0.21	0.05	0.18
Uttar Pradesh	3756	2221	0.13	0.03	0.07
West Bengal	647	164	0.07	0.01	0.018
TOTAL (16 states only)	70042	44983			

states, where livestock rearing is an important activity, also have larger common pastures this adds to CPR area.[20]

2.5 Wasteland and CPR Land

It needs to be understood that the terms CPR land and degraded land arise out of two alternative classifications of land area. Wastelands are, in the main, defined as ecological categories (by the National Wastelands Development Board and the National Remote Sensing Agency). The Ministry of Agriculture also adopts a classification based on land productivity. It is true that, historically, the British termed most non-revenue yielding land as 'the wastes'. However, both the NWDB and the NRSA classifications seem to give primacy to the physical characteristics of the land. The NWDB defines wasteland thus, 'Wasteland means degraded land which can be brought under vegetative cover with reasonable effort and which is currently lying as under-utilised land and land which is deteriorating for lack of appropriate water and soil management or on account of natural causes'. Non-forest wasteland, in the NRSA classification, extends to the following kinds of land: salt-affected land, waterlogged land, marshy/swampy land, gullied/ravinous land, land with and without scrub, sandy area, barren, stony and sheet rock area, mining and industrial waste and snow-covered area. Correspondingly, within forest area, degraded forest and forest blanks are classified as wasteland by the NRSA reckoning. Clearly, these characteristics are independent of either the revenue-yielding nature of the land or the nature of property rights that exist on it. It is just possible, by this definition, that privately-owned revenue generating land (in a canal command, for instance) be a part of wasteland.

Land may be laid waste for a number of reasons, one among them, the nature of property rights on it. The unstated assumption is often that lands with open access or with poorly defined common access are more likely to be laid waste. Be that as it may, it is clear that CPR land and wasteland define two separate, albeit partly overlapping, sets. The existence of common or open access to a certain land is neither a necessary nor a sufficient condition for its being low productivity wasteland.[21]

Table 2.4 gives estimates of CPR land and of wasteland in the 16 major states being considered. Total wasteland is taken as estimated by NWDB to be 129.57 million hectares of which 93.69 are non-forest wasteland. A recent set of data comes from NRSA. This data set is comparable with the NWDB data as it is based on ecological categories. However, it seems to yield a much lower estimate of wastelands as compared to the NWDB estimates. Since the two estimates refer to different points in time, a comparison would suggest that source, the total degraded forest area has come down from 35.89 to 16.3 million hectares and non-forest degraded area from 93.69 to 44.39 million hectares at the all-India level.[22] Since this is highly unlikely in the short span of time separating the two estimates, there is reason to believe that the under-estimation arises out of different estimational procedures.

Table 2.4 gives our estimates of CPRs together with NRSA estimates of wasteland. It is clear that wasteland in a state may be more or less than CPR land. Use of inappropriate technology on private agricultural land, for instance, may result in waterlogging or salinity rendering it into wasteland. In any exercise such as ours that seeks to

TABLE 2.4
Comparative Statistics on CPRs and Wastelands

State	Total CPR (000' HA)	Non-forest CPR (000' HA)	Total Wasteland (000' HA)
Andhra Pradesh	5989	4624	5932
Bihar	5267	2850	2474
Gujarat	3269	2707	4189
Haryana	190	44	357
Himachal Pradesh	5188	1619	1069
Jammu & Kashmir	278	278	3714
Karnataka	3207	2203	2680
Kerala	331	207	163
Madhya Pradesh	13890	6446	8872
Maharashtra	8039	5926	6209
Orissa	4882	1537	2045
Punjab	359	73	370
Rajasthan	11977	11697	9605
Tamil Nadu	2773	2387	2272
Uttar Pradesh	3756	2221	5007
West Bengal	647	164	435
Total (16 States only)	70042	44983	57438

Source: Wasteland data is from NRSA (1989).

examine the links between nature of property rights and degradation and demographic variables, the focus is on CPR land and not on wasteland per se.

From the perspective of grassroots interventions, it is important to distinguish between land that is of intrinsically low capability, land that gets degraded due to technological factors and land that gets degraded due to the absence of well-spelt out property rights. Table 2.5 gives estimates of these two categories of land.

TABLE 2.5
Degraded Land and CPR Land (000' HA)

	Forest Land	Non-forest Land	Total
CPR	25712	48861	74579
Wasteland	18088	44390	60663

It is found that, at the national level, wasteland is of a lower magnitude than CPR land. Considering that some of this wasteland falls within privately-owned land, commonly-owned wasteland is a subset of CPR land. This conclusion is strengthened when we look at CPR and wasteland within forests. Here, wasteland is only about 75 per cent of forest land to which common property rights may exist. When we note that forest blanks (included in wasteland) may exist as management devices in reserve forests, the conclusion that some CPR land is indeed of high productivity seems inescapable (a lower bound estimate of such land of 14.5 million hectares is feasible).

2.6 A Comparison with Alternative Estimates

The methodology followed in arriving at the above estimates of CPR land is essentially one of reclassification of land use statistics, supplemented by data from the Agricultural Censuses and from satellite imagery. This is perhaps, inescapable if the aim is to build-up a comparative macro-level picture for different states and different points of time. It would, however, be useful to compare the estimates obtained by using this approach with those obtained from village-level studies based on the participant observer method. Jodha's study (1986) of CPRs in the dryland regions of India provides one such exhaustive set of estimates. His estimates are based on intensive village-level surveys in 21 districts in seven states. Perhaps those estimates are more precise for the villages to which they refer than any conceivable estimates derived from secondary state-level data. Also, even in the states to which they apply (as they refer only to dry tropical regions), they are likely to be lower than those estimated in this study. This is because Jodha's data leaves out, by definition, those regions where the forest cover is higher. In at least four of the seven states considered by Jodha, protected and unclassed forests form a considerable part of the forest area. To make the two estimates comparable, CPR area—net of protected and unclassed forests—shall be considered for the states studied by Jodha as shown in Table 2.6.

TABLE 2.6
CPR Area in the Dry Tropical Regions (As Per Cent of Total Geographical Area)

State	Jodha's Estimates	Non-forest CPR from Table 2.2 (1990–91)
Andhra Pradesh	10.80	14
Gujarat	11.00	11
Karnataka	16.33	11
Madhya Pradesh	24.14	15
Maharashtra	14.70	19
Rajasthan	14.10	34
Tamil Nadu	10.30	18

We find that the two sets of estimates seem to deviate from each other. A case existed for an estimation at the country level. The NSS in its 54th round (1998) has taken an initiative in estimating CPR land per household across the country. Using a restricted 'de jure' approach, preliminary estimates[23] indicate that on an average, in India, CPR land constitutes 15 per cent of geographical area. It varies from 1 per cent in Punjab to 22 per cent in Rajasthan. It is interesting to note that these broad orders of magnitude and inter-state variations agree with our estimates based on reclassification of land use statistics. In addition to area, the crucial role played by CPRs in providing goods and services to vulnerable sections of the rural poor has also been commented on the NSS (1999) does not estimate the magnitude of dependence of poor rural households on CPRs. However, the percentage of all households dependent on CPRs is estimated and the results are somewhat comparable to those obtained earlier by Jodha

(1986). While the NSS report states that 45 per cent of all rural households in India collect fuelwood from CPRs, Jodha states that 100 per cent of poor rural households depend on CPRs for fuelwood, fodder or food in the seven states he studied. The NSS finds that 48 per cent of all rural households in India report some collection from CPRs. While the average value of this collection is not high, 58 per cent of it consists of fuelwood.

In comparing these two estimates, it must be remembered that the NSS estimates are for 1998 whereas Jodha's estimates are for the mid-eighties. A decline in CPR area and dependence on it is expected. The evidence that exists seems to indicate, however, that due to the operation of market forces and institutional change, there has been a steady decline in the area and quality of CPRs. The decline in CPR institutions is the result of an increase in population and livestock pressures, raising the commercial values of its products, and leading to its subsequent privatisation. Additionally, it is claimed that state-initiated programmes of land distributions have, at times, distributed common lands thereby accentuating the process.

2.7 Some Policy Conclusions

This chapter arrives at estimates of the two sets of CPR land and wasteland using data from alternative sources. While differences of definition and methodology result in variations in estimates, it is clear that the category of CPR land is indeed a quantitative significant one in many parts of the country. In addition, there is evidence that some of it is indeed not wasteland. There does exist scope, therefore, for meaningful grassroots intervention on land producing less than it is capable of. Such interventions can take the form of correct specification of property rights institutions.

For purposes of analysis and policy formulation on the basis of magnitude of CPR land and the ratio of wastelands in CPRs, the country may be divided into the following regions:

1. The tribal hill-states of the North-East: Common property institutions play a very important part in their economies. In these states, land records of so-called private land are not complete mainly because private ownership constitutes an alien category in some areas.

2. The agriculturally-developed states where common property in land seems very small in relation to the total and private property in land, and the related assets are the basis of development: Here, the significance of CPR land would depend on its distributional impact, i.e., on its significance for the livelihood of the rural poor, in particular, in the context of instability in the agricultural output from year to year.
3. The less-developed dry tropical regions of India where CPR land may range from 10 per cent to 20 per cent of the geographical area. These regions are deficient in rainfall, and institutions for promoting better use of CPR land have a great role to play in improving productivity of marginal lands, and in providing employment and livelihood to the rural poor.
4. The relatively high rainfall regions where a large part of CPR land may be forest land: Here, environmental preservation may become an important objective requiring the creation of more efficient institutions, within and outside of state control.

APPENDIX I

Definition of Nine-fold Land Use Classification Classes Mapped Using Ground-based Techniques

Geographical Area

The latest figure of geographical area for the State/Union Territory/District as furnished by the Central Statistical Organisation based on the Surveyor General of India's data should only be used.

Reporting Area for Land Utilisation Purposes

The reporting area stands for the area for which data on land use classification of area are available. In areas where land utilisation figures are based on land records, reporting area is the area according to village papers, i.e., the papers prepared by the village accountants. In some cases, the village papers are not prepared for forest areas but the magnitude of such areas is known. Also, there are tracts in many states for which no village papers exist but for which ad hoc estimates of classification of area, etc., are framed to complete the coverage. In such cases, reporting area should give the summation of the areas for which village papers actually exist and the area for which ad hoc estimates are available.

1. *Forest:* Area under forest includes all lands classed as forests under any legal enactment dealing with forests or administered as forests, whether state-owned or private, and whether wooded or maintained as potential forest land. The area of crop raised in the forests and grazing lands or areas open for grazing within the forest should remain included under the forest area.
2. *Land Put to Agricultural Uses:* This stands for all lands occupied by buildings, road and railways or under water, e.g., rivers and other lands put to use other than agriculture.
3. *Barren and Unculturable Land:* This covers all barren and unculturable land like mountains, deserts. Land which cannot be brought under cultivation unless at a high cost shall be classed as unculturable, whether such land is in isolated blocks or within cultivated holdings.
4. *Permanent Pastures and Other Grazing Lands:* These cover all grazing lands whether they are permanent pastures and meadows or not. Village common grazing lands, permanent pastures shall be included under this head.
5. *Land Under Miscellaneous Tree-crops and Groves Not Included in the Net Area Sown:* Under this class is included all cultivable land which is not included 'net area sown' (but is put to some agricultural use).

Lands under Casaurina trees, thatching grass, bamboo bushes and other groves for fuel, etc., which are not included under orchards, shall be classed under this category.

6. *Culturable Waste:* These include all lands available for cultivation whether or not taken up for cultivation or taken up for cultivation once but not cultivated during current year and last five years or more in succession. Such lands may be either fallow or covered with shrubs and jungles which are not put to any use (they may be assessed or unassessed and may be in isolated blocks or within cultivated holdings). Land once cultivated but not cultivated for five years in succession shall be included in this category at the end of the five years.

7. *Fallow Other than Current Fallows:* This implies all lands which were taken up for cultivation but are temporarily out of cultivation for a period of not less than one year and not more than five years. The reasons for keeping such lands fallow may be one of the following: (i) poverty of cultivators; (ii) inadequate supply of water; (iii) malarial climate; (iv) silting of canal and rivers and (v) unremunerative nature farming.

8. *Current Fallows:* This class comprises cropped areas which are kept fallow during the current year. For example, if any seedling area is not cropped again in the same year, it may be treated as current fallow.

9. *Net Area Sown (NAS):* This represents the area sown with crops and orchards counting areas sown more than once in the same year only once.

Source: Directorate of Economics and Statistics, Department of Agriculture and Cooperation, Ministry of Agriculture, Government of India, New Delhi.

APPENDIX II

Definition of Land Use/Land Cover Categories Mapped Using Remote Sensing Techniques[24]

1. *Built-up Land:* It is defined as an area of human habitation developed due to non-agricultural use and that which has a cover of buildings, transport, communication, utilities in association with water vegetation and vacant lands.

Agricultural Land

It is defined as the land primarily used for farming and for production of food, fibre, other commercial and horticultural crops. It includes land under crops (irrigated and un-irrigated), fallow, plantations, etc.

2. *Crop Land:* It includes those lands with standing crop (per-se) as on the date of the satellite imagery. The crops may be either Kharif (June-September) or Rabi (October-March) or Kharif+Rabi seasons.
3. *Fallow Land:* It is described as agricultural land which is taken up for cultivation but is temporarily allowed to rest, un-cropped for one or more seasons, but not less than one year. These lands are particularly those which are seen devoid of crops at the time when the imagery is taken of both seasons.
4. *Plantations:* It is described as an area under agricultural tree-crops, planted adopting certain agricultural management techniques. It includes tea, coffee, rubber, coconut, arecanut, citrus, orchards and other horticultural nurseries.

Forest

It is an area (within the notified forest boundary) bearing an association predominantly of trees and other vegetation types capable of producing timber and other forest produce.

5. *Evergreen/Semi-evergreen Forest:* It is described as a forest which comprises thick and dense canopy of tall trees which predominantly remain green throughout the year. It includes both coniferous and tropical broad leaved evergreen trees. Semi-evergreen forest is a mixture of both deciduous and evergreen trees but the latter predominate.
6. *Deciduous Forest:* It is described as a forest which predominantly comprises deciduous species and where the trees shed their leaves once in a year.

7. *Degraded Forest or Scrub:* It is described as a forest where the vegetative (crown) density is less than 20 per cent of the canopy cover. It is the result of both biotic and abiotic influences. Scrub is a stunted tree or bush/shrub.
8. *Forest Blank:* It is described as openings amidst forests without any tree cover. It includes openings of assorted sizes and shapes as seen on the imagery.
9. *Forest Plantations:* It is described as an area of trees of species of forestry importance and raised on notified forest lands. It includes Eucalyptus, Casuarina, bamboo etc.
10. *Mangrove:* It is described as a dense thicket or woody aquatic vegetation or forest cover occurring in tidal waters, near estuaries and along the confluence of delta in coastal areas. It includes species of the genera Rhizophora and Avicennia.

Wastelands

It is described as degraded land which can be brought under vegetative cover with reasonable effort and which is currently under-utilised and land which is deteriorating due to lack of appropriate water and soil management or on account of natural causes. Wastelands can result from inherent/imposed constraints such as by location, environment, chemical and physical properties of the soil or financial or management constraints (NWDB 1987).

11. *Salt-affected Land:* The salt-affected land is generally characterised as the land that has adverse effects on the growth of most plants due to the action or presence of excess soluble or high exchangeable sodium. Alkaline land has an exchangeable sodium percentage (ESP) of about 15 which is generally considered as the limit between normal and alkali soils. The predominant salts are carbonates and bicarbonates of sodium. Coastal saline soils may be with or without ingress or inundation by sea water.
12. *Waterlogged Land:* Waterlogged land is that land where the water is at/or near the surface and water stands for most of the year. Such lands usually occupy topographically low-lying areas. It excludes lakes, ponds and tanks.
13. *Marshy/Swampy Land:* Marshy land is that which is permanently or periodically inundated by water and is characterised by vegetation which includes grasses and weeds. Marshes are classified into salt/brackish or fresh water depending on the salinity of water. These exclude mangroves.
14. *Gullied/Ravinous Land:* The gullies are formed as a result of localised surface, run-off affecting the friable unconsolidated material in the formation of perceptible channels resulting in undulating terrain. The gullies are the first stage of excessive land dissection followed by their

networking which leads to the development of ravinous land. The word 'ravine' is usually associated not with an isolated gully but a network of deep gullies formed generally in thick alluvium and entering a nearby river, flowing much lower than the surrounding high grounds. The ravines are extensive systems of gullies developed along river courses.

15. *Land With or Without Scrub:* They occupy (relatively) higher topography like uplands or high grounds with or without scrub. These lands are generally prone to degradation or erosion. These exclude hilly and mountainous terrain.

16. *Sandy Area (coastal and desertic):* These are the areas which have stabilised accumulations of sand in situ or transported in coastal river or inland (desert) areas. These occur in the form of sand dunes, beaches, channel (river/stream) islands, etc.

17. *Barren Rocky/Stony Waste/Sheet Rock Area:* It is defined as the rock exposures of varying lithology, often barren and devoid of soil cover and vegetation and not suitable for cultivation. They occur amidst hill forests as openings or scattered as isolated exposures or loose fragments of boulders or as sheet rocks on plateau and palins. It includes quarry or gravel pit or brick kilns.

Water Bodies

It is an area of impounded water, areal in extent and often with a regulated flow of water. It includes man-made reservoirs/lakes/tanks/canals besides natural lakes, rivers/streams and creeks.

18. *River/Stream:* It is a natural course of flowing water on the land along definite channels. It ranges from a small stream to a big river and its branches. It may be perennial or non-perennial.

19. *Reservoir/Lakes/Tanks/Canal:* It is a natural or man-made enclosed water body with a regulated flow of water. Reservoirs are larger than tanks/lakes and are used for generating electricity, irrigation and for flood control. Tanks are smaller in areal extent with limited use than the former. Canals are inland waterways used for irrigation and sometimes for navigation.

Others

It includes all those which can be treated as miscellaneous because of their nature of occurrence, physical appearance and other characteristics.

20. *Shifting Cultivation:* It is the result of cyclic land use practice of felling trees and burning forest areas for growing crops. Such lands are

also known as Jhum lands. This results in extensive loss of soil leading to land degradation.
21. *Grassland/Grazing Land:* It is an area of land covered with natural grass along with other vegetation often grown for fodder to feed cattle and other animals. Such lands are found in river beds, on uplands, hill slopes, etc. Such lands can also be called permanent pastures or meadows. Grazing lands are those where certain pockets of land are fenced for allowing cattle to graze.
22. *Snow-covered/Glacial Area:* It is defined as a solid form of water consisting of minute particles of ice. It includes permanently snow-covered areas on the Himalayas. Glacier is a mass of accumulated ice occurring amidst permanently snow-covered areas.
23. *Mining/Industrial Waste:* It is an area associated with mining or Industry with excavated material or waste dumps or storage dumps of earthen material or industrial material. Such waste dumps are sometimes covered with or without vegetation.
24. *Salt Pans:* It is a lowland area close to the sea shore or around salt lakes and lined with compartments filled with saline water and heaps of salt. These are man-made artifacts active or abandoned.
25. *Settlements with Mixed Vegetation:* It is an area associated with settlements amidst plantations like bamboo, banana, arecanut and coconut.

ENDNOTES

1. See for such a definition, Bromley (1989).
2. See the exhaustive account of tank management in Tamil Nadu in Shah et al. (1998).
3. For an excellent documentation, see Cincotti and Pangare (1993).
4. The source for this is the Directorate of Economics and Statistics, Ministry of Agriculture and Cooperation, Government of India. See Annexure I to this chapter for the nine-fold classification.
5. The break-up of total forest area on the basis of legal status and ownership is obtained from the Forest Statistics and from documents of the Forest Survey of India.
6. See The Imperial Gazetteer of India, *The Indian Empire*, vol III.
7. See Government of India: *The Gazetteer of India* (1975).
8. Exceptions to this may also exist in parts of the country, notably the north-east.
9. See Government of India (1989) for the definition and estimates.
10. See Government of India, Department of Space (1995). The estimates of wasteland obtained from these two sources vary considerably. See Kadekodi (1997) for a comparative analysis.
11. For estimates for 1980, see Chopra et al. (1990). The methodology followed here is broadly the same.

12. The north-eastern states are not included in the exercise due to the lack of reliable land records statistics.
13. For details, see Annexure I to this chapter. The data source is Directorate of Economics and Statistics, Ministry of Agriculture and Cooperation, Government of India.
14. Agricultural Census data are treated as most authentic as they are based on a complete enumeration of all holdings in all states in India. To arrive at the state-level figures on land owned from the Agricultural Census, the category—land wholly owned—is added to the category—partly-land owned—as obtained from partly-owned and partly-rented land.
15. The decrease is explicable in terms of the population pressure and the consequent demand for land. The increase is probably due to the larger magnitude of land reportedly left fallow in states such as Tamil Nadu.
16. This may involve some over-estimation of CPRs, as 'protected and unclassed forests' includes privately-owned pastures.
17. To refer briefly to the controversy around estimates of the total forest area in the country: According to forest statistics, which is based on land use and legal status data, 74.86 million hectares comprising 22.73 per cent of the geographical area can be classified as forest area. The corresponding figure given by the first figures from National Remote Sensing Agency (based on satellite data for 1980–82) is 46.35 million hectares comprising 14.10 per cent of the geographical area. The discrepancy is basically due to differences in methods of data collection and definitions of status. In the late eighties, an exercise was carried out by the Forest Survey to attempt a reconciliation of the two data sources by undertaking a critical comparison of their respective methodologies. For the late eighties, we have used this source. It depends, by and large, on satellite data. We are aware, however, that estimates can differ due to alternative methods of interpreting this data and to the presence or otherwise, of ground-truthing.
18. Some of the states in this category may also have large tribal belts; the over-estimation in the case of Rajasthan may, however, be only partly true. See Jodha's estimate of CPR area in Rajasthan as a percentage of geographical area in table 2.4.
19. These estimates are from Kadekodi (1997).
20. It is all the more well known that the extent of variation in CPR will be still higher.
21. This issue is discussed exhaustively in Kadekodi and Perwaiz (1998). They also give comparative estimates of the two categories of land.
22. See Kadekodi and Perwaiz (1998) for a discussion on the two data-sets on wasteland, the one from NWDB and the one from NRSA.
23. See NSS (1999) 54th Round, Draft Report No. 452 (54/3.3/31).
24. See Government of India (1995).

Chapter 3

Population Movements, Environmental Degradation and Property Rights: A District-level Analysis

3.1 A District-level Study of Arid and Semi-arid Regions

The previous chapter concludes that land on which common property rights exist, is of considerable magnitude in India. Non-forest land of this kind is in the range of 40–45 million hectares. Additionally, forest land also permits access of different kinds—access, which can rightly be referred to as common. Such common property resources are quantitatively more significant in the arid and semi-arid regions of India. Further, these regions also record high levels of out-migration. This chapter studies the linkages between population movements, environmental degradation (viewed primarily as deforestation and land degradation), and the role of property rights or institutional structures ensuring such rights in the arid and semi-arid agricultural zones of India. In other words, it addresses the question: is it true that with the creation of well-defined property rights as a consequence of appropriate institutional arrangements, labour moves towards the creation of common assets and an improvement in the environment takes place? Out-migration is prevented and higher levels of population are supported by the same resources.

The hypothesis stated above can be tested in a number of ways. Two possible alternatives are: an econometric analysis of a large database extracted from secondary data, and the study of indepth experiments in property rights changes in smaller areas. Both approaches have been attempted in this volume. This chapter highlights the interlinkages through analysis of a large cross-sectional data set primarily because it is amenable to econometric analysis. This secondary data-based study captures the quantitative aspects of the relationship between out-migration, environmental degradation and the existence of common resources.

The methodology consists of the following steps:

- Variables representing different aspects of migration, natural resource base and degradation are identified for the study region comprising 89 districts in the arid and semi-arid regions of India.
- Key dimensions representing aspects to be studied are represented by carefully constructed variables. A semi-quantitative analysis of the relations between them is obtained using factor analysis.
- A simultaneous structural system is formulated and estimated through the system method of estimation to highlight the interlinkages between the two key dimensions and arrive at the short and long run effects of exogenous variables on the endogenous or response variables. It is expected that possible changes in the nature of the relationship between internal migration and efficacy of common property regimes will be thrown up.

Section 3.2 gives a brief introduction to the study region and section 3.3 categorises the variables selected for analysis. Sections 3.4 and 3.5 use the techniques of factor analysis and a simultaneous equations system to test the hypothesis and section 3.6 summarises results and derives policy implications.

3.2 The Study Region

The arid and semi-arid regions in the western and central parts of India are defined to include three zones from the Indian Planning Commission's agro-climatic classification of India.[1] From the viewpoint of administrative units, 89 districts falling in the central and western part of India constitute the study area. The initial selection of an ecological unit for analysis is a consequence of the contention that livelihood systems tend to be built around ecological reality in the absence of outside interventions. Links with the outside economy must take this reality into account. However, the econometric analysis is carried out at the more desegregated district level.

The Central Plateau and Hill region (Agro-climatic Zone 8) consists of 46 districts from three states. The zone is interspersed with plateau and hill areas, the physiography being characterised by:

(a) Low hill ranges, mounds, narrow valleys with acute soil erosion and excessive run-off.
(b) Undulating topography.
(c) Vast areas of barren and uncultivated land.

This zone has a geographical area of 37,592.6 hectares, i.e., it accounts for 11.6 per cent of the land mass of India but it is home to only 8 per cent of its population with a density of 136 persons per sq. km. The annual rainfall ranges from 490 mm to 1570 mm. The 16 districts that fall in the state of Rajasthan have an annual rainfall of 500 mm/or less. The sub-region of western Madhya Pradesh has, however, rainfall of about 1570 mm.

Per capita availability of forest area is 0.14 hectares, per capita net sown area is about 0.33 hectares with irrigated area being 0.07 hectares per capita. The major source of irrigation is wells and tubewells, which irrigate 55 per cent of the area. Canals and tanks come second with 36 per cent. Forests cover 20.17 per cent of the reported area with variations between 4.2 per cent and 38.86 per cent. The livestock to man ratio is 1.04 with cattle population comprising a large component, and with variations between sub-regions. While the northern hills support only 1.9 per cent of the total livestock population, the southern plains and the semi-arid eastern plains support 27 per cent.

The Western Plateau and Hill Region (Agro-climatic Zone 9) comprises 34 districts from the three states of Rajasthan, Madhya Pradesh and Maharashtra with a geographical area of 33,221.97 hectares. It has a population of 56.13 million with a density of 169 per sq. km. The river basins are hilly and narrow in the west, and broad and flat in the east. The rainfall varies between 580 mm and 1176 mm with an average of 904 mm. More than 70 per cent of the area is either medium or deep black soil with high clay content and poor drainage. The net sown area is 65 per cent of the geographic area with little variation. Per capita net sown area is 0.385 hectares, with 11.5 per cent on an average being irrigated. Wells account for 71.3 per cent, canals 25 per cent and tanks 3.7 per cent of this irrigated area. Forests occupy 11.3 per cent of the geographical area with lands not available for cultivation constituting about 8.77 per cent. Livestock population per hectare of gross sown area is 1.7, with cattle contributing 54 per cent, buffaloes 13 per cent and sheep and goats 29.78 per cent of total livestock population.

The Western Dry Region (Agro-climatic Zone 14) consists of nine districts of Rajasthan, with a geographical area of 17,580 hectares. The average rainfall is 395 mm with a very high year-to-year fluctuation. The population is 13.3 million and the density is 58.16 persons per sq. km. The zone has all the characteristics of hot desert, namely, scanty and erratic rainfall, high evaporation, non-existence of perennial rivers and sparse vegetation. The ground water table is often deep and very brackish. The soils are desertic with excessive permeability and low moisture-holding capacity. The average land to man ratio is high with net sown are per person 0.750 hectares. However, only 6.3 per cent of net sown area is irrigated.

Ground water is the major source of irrigation accounting for 92 per cent of the net irrigated area. The forest cover is very poor at 7.28 per cent of the geographical area and land designated as waste is

TABLE 3.1
Characteristics of Agro-climatic Zones

	Units	Zone 8	Zone 9	Zone 14
Geographical Area	Thousand hectares	37592.6	33221.9	17580
Rainfall (annual average)	mm	1030	904	395
Density of Population	Persons per sq. km	136.77	169.28	58.16
New Sown Area per capita	Hectares	0.33	0.385	0.75
Forest Area	Per cent of total area	20.17	11.3	7.28
Irrigated Area	Per cent of net sown area	21.2	11.5	6.3
Livestock Density	Animals per hectare of GCA	2.64	1.77	2.32
Sheep and Goats	Per cent of livestock	36.41	29.78	72

Note: GCA is gross cropped area, i.e. net sown area corrected for cropping intensity.

23.1 per cent. Livestock density is 2.32 animals per hectare of gross sown area and 1.87 animals per person. Sheep and goats constitute 72 per cent of livestock population, and cattle and buffaloes share just one-fourth.

3.3 Selection of Variables

Three basic blocks of variables are identified for analysis at the district level: demographic, developmental and environmental. Demographic changes are characterised by size, growth, distribution and movements of population over the seventies and eighties. Developmental patterns are captured by changes in the structure and pattern of employment. The data pertains to composition of workers employed in different sectors such as agriculture, factories, mining and quarrying, over the last two decades. Similarly, environmental degradation has been represented by livestock composition over the seventies and eighties and changes therein have been selected to characterise resource degradation patterns. Changes in patterns of use of natural resources like land, water and forests also supplement the above.

The data-base for econometric analysis for the study are primarily drawn from CMIE reports (1982, 1987), Agro-climatic Zonal Profiles from Planning Commission (1982, 1993), Census Reports of 1981 and 1991, Series of Occasional Papers from Registrar General's Office (1989, 1987), Ministry of Health and Family Welfare Reports (1987) and Ministry of Environment and Forests, Government of India (1991). Most of the basic data pertains to the mid-seventies and mid-eighties and structural changes in the basic indicators over the period are utilised for getting some insights into complex nature of linkages between different blocks of characteristics over the period.

3.3.1 Demographic Variables

While net immigration at the country level may be insignificant, interregional migration assumes significance in an analysis at the meso- and micro-levels (zonal, state, district or block, etc.). However, non-availability of data on such basic demographic parameters as fertility, mortality and migrational movements at district level, renders the task of characterising population movements at this level difficult. Thus, we used composite indices depicting natural and net migrational component for all the 369 districts of India for which the relevant data was available around the beginning of the eighties.

The composite indices were built using data pertaining to 10 different socio-economic and demographic indicators, viz., crude birth rate (DCBR), probability of dying before the age of 2 (DPDA), per cent married females in age group 15–19 (DPMF), couple protection rate (DCPR), population density (DDEN), per cent literate (DLIT), per cent urban (DURB), per cent agricultural workers (DAGW), average daily employment in factories per lakh population (DEFP) and sex ratio (DSER). In other words, demographic parameters and socio-economic variables determining population growth and its redistribution process have been used to determine the natural and migrational growth potential of the population. The elicited factor structure and factor score coefficients for evolving the composite indices describing the two components of population growth, viz., Natural Growth Potential (NGP) and Migrational Growth Potential (MGP), are presented in Appendix Table A3.1.

The data on 10 other demographic indicators depicting growth, distribution and redistribution aspects of population over the eighties and nineties for the 89 districts comprising the three agro-climatic regions over arid and semi-arid zones of India is included in the study. Furthermore, data on the extent of literacy and urbanisation during 1981 and 1991 for the same 89 districts is also included in the study. The list of the selected demographic, urbanisation and literacy variables and their summary statistics depicting spectrum of inter-district variations over the three agro-climatic regions are provided in Appendix Tables A3.2 and A3.3 respectively.

3.3.2 *Natural Resource Variables*

Structural changes in land utilisation patterns seem to characterise well the extent of land degradation or upgradation over time. The composition of land use may also reflect changes in property rights patterns as discussed earlier with regard to the continuum of property rights. Generally, forest land is state-owned in India whereas net sown area is largely private-owned. Thus, to some extent, changes in the composition of land use patterns can identify the changes in the property rights over a period. The list of land related variables characterising its availability and usage patterns over the seventies and eighties is provided in the Appendix Table A3.2. Summary statistics depicting spectrum of inter-district variations over the three agro-climatic regions is provided in Appendix Table A3.3. The land resource related variables pertain to total geographical area, net sown area, forest area and dense forest-covered area for all the 89 districts for two points of time over the seventies and eighties.

Water availability and the extent of its usage seem to be important factors influencing all agricultural and agriculture-related activities such as cattle rearing, generation or regeneration of pastures and afforestation. Assured availability of water and its proper harvesting becomes increasingly important in water-scarcity regions such as arid and semi-arid zones under the purview of the present study.

Water harvesting activities such as building of anicuts or nullah-bunding are also linked with the availability of water. A list of water related variables depicting its availability and usage patterns is provided in the Appendix Table 3.3. The data pertain to annual normal rainfall, and gross irrigated area as per cent of gross cropped area for two points of time over the seventies and eighties.

3.3.3 Livestock Related Variables

Changes in livestock population have often been postulated to result from the forest degradation process which in turn affects the fodder availability situation for rearing of livestock. Sheep and goats tend to substitute cattle with increase in degradation. It can be argued that the changed composition of livestock, especially an increased proportion of sheep and goats in total livestock, accelerates the process of deforestation and land degradation or desertification. The study has selected some livestock related variables over two different points of time over seventies and eighties, to gain insight into some such issues. The data pertains to the number of sheeps and goats and cattle population for all the districts under study. The list of selected variables and summary statistics depicting spectrum of dispersions over the three regions is provided in Appendix Tables A3.2 and A3.3.

3.3.4 Employment Related Variables

Distress migration from rural to urban areas is caused because of lack of employment opportunities in economically backward agricultural tracts and better employment opportunities in industrial and urban centres in surrounding areas. Thus, rural out-migration to urban and industrially developed centres stems from push factors at the place of origin. Urban amenities and better employment opportunities act as the pull factors at the place of destination for these rural out-migrants. We have selected some employment related variables to depict changes in the composition of agricultural, industrial and mining and quarrying sectors. The list of selected variables and summary statistics depicting inter-district variations over the selected regions is provided in the Appendix Tables A3.2 and A3.3.

3.4 Factor Analysis of Interlinkages between Population Movements, Environmental Degradation and Property Rights

Semi-quantitative insights into the structural linkages between population movements, environmental degradation and delineation of property rights are captured through a factor analysis based on secondary data for the arid and semi-arid agricultural zones of India comprising 89 districts in the study region. This section highlights structural linkages between population movements, developmental patterns and environmental degradation patterns in arid and semi-arid regions in the western and central parts of India. Panel data on district profiles for the key characteristics identifying the crucial dimensions for the purpose would have been ideal for highlighting the exact nature of linkages. Nevertheless, non-availability of data even on the basic characteristics is dealt with by resorting to proxy variables characterising the key dimensions.

The factor analysis approach starts with the correlation matrix for the original variables and elicits principal factors accounting for inter-district variations among the variables, in descending order of magnitude (Harman, 1960). The principal factor solution, depicting key dimensions of the integrated structure of interconnected variables, is further subjected to orthogonal rotation to evolve simple and meaningful factor structures. It may be noted here that the interchange of positions of rotated factors alongwith other parameters have no bearing on the composition or interpretation of the factor structure. Additional advantage with factor analytical approach is that it takes care of missing data by first estimating missing data correlation matrix (MDC), in which correlations are worked out on pair-wise observations on the corresponding variables for different districts. In other words, maximum information on the selected variables gets utilised. The correlation matrix, in turn, becomes an input for eliciting factor structures.

3.4.1 *Factor Structure*

The rotated factor structure of the 17 variables is presented in Table 3.2. Perusal of the first factor (F-I) reveals strong linkage between depletion of common land area (CCLA) and agricultural productivity (CFGP). In districts with potentials for improvements in agricultural productivity as measured by increase in per capita food grain production, the depletion of common land areas, largely comprising of wastelands and pasturelands, is expected to be higher. Privatisation of common land is possibly taking place. Also, we find that population growth is relatively higher as depicted by higher and positive factor loading of the population growth variable (DPGE). Furthermore, the extent of net immigration in such districts is also higher as depicted by relatively lower but positive factor loading of migrational index (DMGP).

Perusal of the second factor (F-II) reveals that in districts where depletion of forest-covered area (CFCA) is high, the growth in the number of sheep and goats (CNSA) is also high. Thus, forest degradation or depletion of forest area seems to be positively associated with increase in number of sheep and goats. Furthermore, it may be of interest to mention that depletion of forest resources seems to be less in high rainfall areas as depicted by relatively higher and similar signs of factor loadings of the two variables, viz., changes in forest area (CFCA) and annual normal rainfall (DANR).

A perusal of the third factor (F-III) reveals that distress out-migration from rural to urban areas as depicted by higher factor loading of change in rural sex ratio in favour of females (CRSR), is faster in districts where compositional changes in livestock have gone in favour of sheep and goats (CPSG), depicting forest degradation or depletion of forest-covered

TABLE 3.2
Varimax Rotated Factor Structure

Variable	Factor Loading on Variables					Communality
	F-I	F-II	F-III	F-IV	F-V	
Demographic						
1. DPGE	0.55	0.49	0.11	0.24	0.27	0.68
2. DNGP	0.12	−0.05	−0.01	0.85	−0.25	0.81
3. DMGP	0.24	0.16	0.06	−0.82	−0.05	0.77
4. CDEN	0.73	0.08	0.07	−0.09	0.04	0.56
5. CRSR	0.01	0.04	0.97	−0.05	−0.02	0.95
6. CLTR	−0.19	−0.01	0.04	0.78	0.05	0.65
Water related						
7. DANR	0.15	−0.76	−0.05	−0.15	0.25	0.69
8. DGIS	−0.07	0.12	−0.01	−0.01	−0.82	0.69
9. CIRI	−0.06	−0.07	−0.06	0.13	0.64	0.44
10. CFGP	0.76	−0.21	−0.09	−0.22	−0.12	0.69
Employment						
11. CAWM	−0.03	−0.07	−0.02	0.18	−0.55	0.34
12. CADE	0.30	0.017	0.14	0.43	0.14	0.34
13. CWMQ	−0.07	−0.06	−0.08	0.08	−0.04	0.02
Environment						
14. CNSA	−0.03	0.51	−0.07	−0.18	0.20	0.34
15. CPSG	0.06	0.08	−0.98	−0.01	0.03	0.97
16. CFCA	−0.13	−0.48	0.06	0.05	0.20	0.30
17. CCLA	−0.55	0.51	0.01	−0.09	0.08	0.58
Eigen Values	1.92	1.63	2.06	2.53	1.69	

area. In other words, an increase in the proportion of sheep and goats to total livestock is found to accompany out-migration of male workers to surrounding industrial and service centres in search of jobs. Both are indicators of environmental degradation.

The fourth factor (F-IV) is primarily constituted by demographic variables, where population growth and its constituents, viz., natural (DNGP) and migrational (DMGP) components, are well connected as per general expectations. Also, we find that improvements in qualitative aspects of population in terms of literacy (CLTR) are positively associated with improvements in employment in factories (CADE). Thus, linkages among most of the constituents of the factor seem to be consistent with general expectations.

A perusal of the fifth factor (F-V) reveals that extent of irrigation in the rural tracts is positively associated with employment of agricultural workers. In other words, assured water supply or higher irrigational intensity (DGIS) provides assured employment to agricultural workers (CAWM) and may be responsible for curtailing distress out-migration of rural male workers. It may be of interest to mention that levels and changes seem to be inversely related as depicted by relatively higher but opposite sign of factor loadings of DGIS and CIRI. This implies that a limit exists to the positive impact of irrigation on employment. Increased productivity of private land cannot be depended upon to absorb higher levels of population, and some other kinds of interventions may be required.

However, most of the interlinkages between groups of variables depicting environmental changes, population movements and redistribution process, employment structural variables depicting developmental patterns, etc., have turned out to be consistent with general expectations. It may be noted here that the semi-quantitative insights provided by the factor analysis provide a basis for formulating a structural system to quantify the structural linkages for further multivariate analysis.

3.5 Simultaneous Structural System

As stated earlier, the nature and strength of linkages between population movement, environmental degradation process and the changing property rights in the region can be studied with the help of a simultaneous equations system. This section examines the interactions by formulating a simultaneous structural system; with rural out-migration, environmental degradation, and property rights over land being treated as endogenous variables in the system, and selected demographic and developmental indicators being treated as exogenous to the system. A priori, the following kinds of interrelationships between levels, changes and inter-spatial movements of population can be identified:

(1) increases in population result in pressures on land and water in rural environments,
(2) environmental degradation of this kind results in so-called 'distress' out-migration from rural tracts,
(3) changing property rights in land and in common property resources can limit or even end stress out-migration from the rural tracts,

(4) a parallel stream of 'developmental' migration occurs as a consequence of employment opportunities in the urban non-agricultural sectors of the economy,
(5) both kinds of migration have their own impact on urban environments as well.

The 'distress' migration referred to in (b) and the 'developmental' migration referred to in (d) are both the consequence of differences in income between the origin and destination regions. As stated earlier, this difference can be affected, in a substantial manner, by the magnitude of income or consumption derived from common property resources and the certainty with which it is available. Further, the present model, while focusing attention on the hitherto neglected area of links between (b) and (c), does not ignore income and wage differentials as an influence on the level of migration. These factors are taken care of by the exogenous variables included in the simultaneous equations framework.

The simultaneous structural system, designed to capture the combined impact of the above-mentioned movements, has four endogenous variables and 11 exogenous variables.

The endogenous variables in the system are:

(1) Environmental Degradation Index measured by change in the structural composition of livestock. An increase in the percentage of sheep and goats in the total livestock is taken to imply a degradation in the environment as these animals survive better in degraded areas (CPSG). This indirect measure of environmental degradation is preferred to more direct measures such as forest degradation and fall in level of ground water because of availability of cross-section and time series data.
(2) Change in private property rights on agricultural land as characterised by change in net sown area to total geographical area over the period 1974 to 1984 (CNSA).
(3) Change in common land area over the same period (CCLA). To arrive at a proxy variable for this, an approximation for usable common access land is obtained for each district by excluding privately-owned and state-owned land and barren and un-cultivable land from the geographical area.[2]

(4) Distress out-migration from rural tracts to towns, urban agglomerations and metropolitan centres because of push factors is approximated by change in sex composition in rural areas in favour of females (CRSR). This is because distress migration is usually male-dominated with the females staying behind and thus changing sex composition would reflect the extent of out-migration from rural areas.

The system also includes 11 exogenous socio-economic and developmental variables. Rainfall, irrigation and land productivity are the weather and agriculture related variables. Employment opportunities provided by industrial development of the intended destination are represented by the extent of non-farm employment activities in factories and in mining and quarrying sectors and by the non-agricultural development index. Areas with a higher degree of non-farm related employment are also likely to have a higher level of urban income. Another exogenous variable, percentage of literate to total population in a given district, also reflects the probability of urban employment since the more literate presumably possess a higher probability of being absorbed in the urban labour force.

The district level non-agricultural development index (DNAD) is derived from 14 selected developmental variables encompassing sectoral aspects of the economic development process at the district level. The index is elicited through multivariate factor analytic technique facilitating weights to be assigned to different developmental variables. The weights are based on factor loadings in the varimax-rotated factor structure of the interrelated developmental variables and the elicited eigen values (Gulati, 1992). Interestingly, the factor loadings of the elicited factor (DNAD) turn out to be relatively much higher on the constituting non-agricultural developmental variables, viz., average daily employment in factories and in household industrial units, extent of urbanisation, extent of electrification and bank advances for industrial activity. Thus, the elicited indices for all the 89 districts reflect the extent of non-agricultural employment potentials in the districts which, in turn, are hypothesised to affect the rural–urban population movements.

It is, therefore, correct to presume that income differentials and probabilities of urban employment as causal factors for migration are being included in the model. Higher demographic pressure on land is represented by population growth and increase in population densities. It can be concluded, therefore, that while our model focuses on the hitherto relatively ignored area of the linkages between migration and common property rights, it does contain exogenous variables that take into account the impact of more traditional influences on migration.

The notation for the variables selected is given in Table 3.3.

TABLE 3.3
List of Selected Variables

Variable Abbreviation	Description of the Variable
CRSR	Change in Rural Sex Ratio to Total Sex Ratio (females per 1000 males)
CPSG	Change in Sheep and Goats as per cent of Total Livestock Population
CNSA	Change in Net Sown Area per 1000 sq. km of Geographical Area
CCLA	Change in Common Land Area as per cent of Geographical Area
DPGE	Population Growth Rate in the Eighties
DNAD	Non-agricultural Development Index
DANR	Average Normal Rainfall
CFCA	Change in Forest-covered Area as per cent of Geographical Area
CFGP	Change in per capita Foodgrain Production
CADE	Change in Average Daily Employment per lakh Population
CWMQ	Change in Workers Employed in Mining and Quarrying per lakh Population
CDEN	Change in Density of Population per sq. km
CIRI	Change in Gross Irrigated Area to Gross Cropped Area
DLTE	Per cent Population Literate in 1981
DFPE	Per capita Food Grain Production in 1980

3.5.1 The Structural Relations

The data used in the study is derived from secondary sources. Most of it is published data obtained from government sources.[3] It is also important to note that a large number of variables are defined as changes between two points of time in the early and the late eighties. The exercise is carried out using these and not panel data, primarily due to non-availability of panel data for all variables used.

The simultaneous structural system hypothesised relationships among variables comprising the four structural relations. The first structural relation depicts the extent of distress rural out-migration as measured by change in rural sex composition in favour of females in relation to the district's sex ratio (CRSR) as a function of:

(a) the environmental degradation variable represented by changes in proportion of sheep and goats to total livestock (CPSG),
(b) change in net sown area to total geographical area (CNSA), and
(c) change in proportion of common land to total geographical area (CCLA).

The following equation defines the above relationship:

$$CRSR = f(CPSG, CNSA, CCLA, CFGP, CADE, CWMQ, DLTE) \qquad (1)$$

The four exogenous variables included in this equation are the land productivity variable, viz., change in per capita food production (CFGP); two non-agricultural employment variables, viz., change in average daily employment in factories per lakh population (CADE) and change in employment in mining and quarrying sector (CWMQ); and a social development variable depicting the district's extent of literacy in the eighties (DLTE).

The independent variables in this equation represent the different factors that impact the out-migration from rural areas, out-migration that is of the 'distress' out-migration variety. Both the push and pull factors are included. Changes in land productivity and in net sown area are expected to have a negative effect on out-migration. Similarly, the environmental degradation process is contended to have a strong positive impact on rural-urban migrational patterns. Among the 'pull' factors, availability of employment opportunities in urban and industrial centres is most significant. The non-agricultural employment variables that have been included in the set of exogenous variables are: the extent of employment in factories (CADE) and employment in mining and quarrying sector (CWMQ). Furthermore, a social development related variable, the extent of literacy in the population (DLTE), is also presumed to have a strong bearing on the migrational flows. It is generally contended that rural out-migrational streams are dominated by younger age groups and relatively more educated adult members to begin with. Subsequently, the adult outmigrants may be followed by other family members comprising spouses and dependants.

The second structural relation postulates environmental degradation (as reflected in change in favour of sheep and goats in the livestock population (CPSG) as a function of two endogenous variables, viz., change in common land area depicting community ownership rights on land (CCLA), distress migration from the rural tracts depicted by excessive change in rural sex composition to overall sex composition (CRSR) and an exogenous variable, viz., change in forest-covered area (CFCA) as given below:

$$CPSG = f(CCLA, CRSR, CFCA) \qquad (2)$$

The exogenous variable has been included as several empirical studies have demonstrated that deforestation in several tracts has gone together with the changing composition of the livestock in favour of sheep and goats. These can be sustained easily by grazing on degraded tracts, unlike other milch animals like cows and buffaloes which require more fodder.

In the third structural relation, change in private ownership of land is measured by change in net sown area to total geographical area (CNSA). It is stated to be a function of one endogenous variable, viz., change in common land to total geographical area (CCLA), to capture the tendency towards privatisation.

$$CNSA = f(CCLA, DANR, CIRI, DFPE, DNAD, CDEN) \qquad (3)$$

The five exogenous variables that are postulated as affecting changes in net sown area are: (*a*) three agricultural variables, viz., annual normal rainfall (DANR), change in irrigational intensity (CIRI) and agricultural land productivity measured by per capita food production (DFPE) and (*b*) two non-agricultural variables, i.e., non-agricultural development index (DNAD) and population pressure on land characterised by change in density of population per sq. km (CDEN).

Change in net sown area is taken to stand for increase in private land ownership. The magnitude of change in private-owned croplands could have a strong inverse relationship with changes in common land areas. On the other hand, improvements in irrigational facilities (themselves sometimes a consequence of protection of common land) and greater availability of rain water are expected to have a strong bearing on land productivity and thus, encourage extension of private property in land by increasing private returns from it. Similarly, higher land productivity or better quality of land also encourages private ownership.

Non-agricultural development in the district may also influence migration outflows and thus land use patterns in the rural tracts. The industrial and tertiary development related out-migrational flows from the areas may influence changing property rights in two ways. By decreasing the pressure of population on land, they lower the need for increased privatisation of land. Simultaneously, this outflow decreases the availability of labour for use on agricultural land and is expected to make it more difficult to manage land.

The fourth structural relation depicts the extent of change in common land area (CCLA) as determined by changes in net sown area (CNSA), changes in forest-covered area (CFCA), improvements in land productivity (CFGP), population growth in the seventies (DPGS), and change in the pressure of population on land (CDEN).

$$CCLA = f(CNSA, CFGP, CFCA, DPGS, CDEN) \qquad (4)$$

Equations (3) and (4) capture the mutual dependence of common and private property resources in the specific context of land. Such interdependence was found to be crucial in the analysis of the motivation for the protection of common land in a number of regions such as the lower Sivaliks (Chopra, Kadekodi and Murty 1990). The realisation that common land provides inputs of water (through increased ground water levels, for instance) and fodder to improve the productivity of privately-owned fields often results in its protection. Such a linkage is often assumed to be reflected in the quality of the common land. Here, the assumption is that area changes with respect to common land will also result as a consequence of this linkage.

Furthermore, the economies of scale factor may bring around private individuals with small land holdings to become a part of a common property scheme of management (WRI, 1995). Small fragments of submarginal land holdings may be uneconomic under private property regimes and may come to be cared for better if institutional change to pool them was made possible. This equation helps us to see whether such tendencies get reflected in the macro-level data.

Land productivity can also be an important determinant of property rights structures over land. A higher level of productivity may result in privatisation of common land. It is because of this that the land productivity variable (CFGP) has been included as one of the determinants of land under common property rights regimes. In a similar vein, demographic pressures on land characterised by extent of population growth (DPGS) and its pressure on land, as represented by change in density (CDEN), have also been included as predictors of landownership patterns.

3.5.2 *Parametric Estimates of the Model*

The functional form of all the four structural relations is assumed to be intrinsically linear, i.e., linear in parameters. A persual of the system reveals that all the structural relations are over-identified and thus the three-stage least squares system estimational procedure (3SLS) is used for eliciting consistent estimates of the structural coefficients. The estimated structural coefficients are presented in Table 3.4. Theoretically, the ordinary least squares (OLS) estimates of the structured parameters are not only biased but also inconsistent (Intriligator, 1980). The system method employed here seems to have eliminated the simultaneity bias and provided consistent estimates. The 3SLS estimates are asymptotically efficient under correct specification conditions. The estimates are discussed below.

A perusal of the parametric estimates in the first column of Table 3.4 reveals that the process of environmental degradation in the arid and semi-arid zones of India has a significant and positive impact on distress rural out-migration. The degradation process accelerates rural out-migration. Another factor depicting significant and negative impact on distress rural out-migration turns out to be changes in common property resources. A decrease in land under common property regimes accelerates the process of distress out-migration from rural areas.

The estimates of the equation for compositional change in livestock (CPSG), a proxy variable for environmental degradation, are presented, in the second column of Table 3.4. Decrease in the area of

TABLE 3.4
3SLS Estimates of the Model

Explanatory Variables	Dependent	Variables		
	(1)	(2)	(3)	(4)
	CRSR	CPSG	CNSA	CCLA
Endogenous				
CRSR	–	0.037* (11.77)	–	–
CPSG	26.639* (13.93)	–	–	–
CNSA	2.055* (0.75)	–	–	–3.554* (3.77)
CCLA	–4.072* (1.98)	–0.174 (2.24)	–0.075* (2.42)	–
Exogenous				
INTERCEPT	–2504.5* (7.61)	83.211* (8.15)	109* (7.09)	594.64* (6.07)
DANR	–	–	0.011* (3.06)	–
CIRI	–	–	0.032* (1.36)	–
DFPE	–	–	0.010* (0.80)	–
CFGP	0.241* (1.13)	–	–	–0.276* (2.47)
CFCA	–	0.003* (0.77)	–	–0.115* (2.82)
CADE	–0.033* (0.68)	–	–	–
CWQM	–0.004* (0.34)	–	–	–
DNAD	–	–	–1.95* (1.93)	–
DPGS	–	–	–	–0.015 (0.02)
CDEN	–	–	–0.035 (0.56)	–0.587* (2.11)
DLTE	–0.314 (.33)	–	–	–
R^2	0.92	0.91	0.49	0.50
$\bar{R}^2$	0.91	0.91	0.45	0.47

Note: * denotes significance at 1 per cent.

common land has a significant and negative impact on environmental degradation process. Alternatively, districts with similar levels of distress out-migration and changes in forest-covered area but with larger land areas under common property rights register lower environmental degradation. Furthermore, higher out-migration from rural tracts also exhibits significant and positive relationship with the environmental degradation process. Thus, higher extent of out-migration from rural tracts ceteris paribus follows from higher environmental degradation in arid and semi-arid zones over western parts of India.

A perusal of the estimates provided in the third column of Table 3.4 reveals that privatisation of land has been at the expense of commonly-owned land. Alternatively, districts with similar levels of agricultural resources, like annual rainfall, land productivity and out-migration potentials but with larger common ownership rights, have shown positive changes in private ownership rights over agricultural land. Possibly, the explanation could be in terms of larger encroachments on commonly-owned land over the period.

Interestingly, higher normal rainfall districts within arid and semi-arid western zones of India have been found to have significantly positive changes in private ownership rights over agricultural tracts. Among the demographic variables, we find that districts with lower non-agricultural development related migrational potential register significantly higher changes in privately-owned croplands. Alternatively, areas with a higher non-agricultural development potential depict much lower changes in privately-owned croplands. When people have fewer alternate sources of livelihood to look forward to in urban areas, they tend to think in terms of expansion of privately-owned land.

The parametric estimates in fourth column of Table 3.4 reveal that changes in common land areas and new sown areas are significantly and negatively associated. Possibly, expansion of privately-owned cultivated lands is at the expense of shrinkage of common land areas. In other words, increases in net sown areas, largely privately-owned, have a significant and negative impact on changes in common land areas. Looked at from another viewpoint, it is seen that districts with lower land productivity have experienced significantly higher improvements in common land areas or common ownership rights over agricultural land. Alternatively, regions with higher improvements in land productivity have depicted significant declines in common land areas.

3.5.3 The Impact Multipliers

The structural coefficients provide estimates of the direct effects of different predictors on the response variables in the system. In other words, solving the simultaneous structural system of four equations for the four endogenous variables, in terms of the exogenous variables, provides the reduced form coefficients of the model. The reduced form coefficient includes interaction effects also and can, therefore, be interpreted as the total effect of the exogenous variable on the endogenous one. In a static model, the reduced form coefficients are the same as impact multipliers.

The estimated impact multipliers are presented in Appendix Table A3.7. The impact multiplier of an exogenous variable upon any endogenous variable is shown in the corresponding cell. For instance, 1 per cent increase in ratio of gross irrigated area to gross cropped area (CIRI) will bring about 0.16 per cent decline in distress out-migration from the rural tracts (CRSR). Also, it will bring about 0.03 per cent decline in proportion of sheep and goats to livestock composition (CPSG) implying an improvement in the environment to that extent. Furthermore, it brings about 0.04 per cent increase in net sown area to total geographical area (CNSA), and 0.15 per cent decline in common land area (CCLA). Interestingly, we find that the total effect of all the agricultural variables on distress rural out-migration is consistent with general expectations. Higher irrigation intensity (CIRI), higher land productivity and changes therein (CFGP) and regeneration of forests (CFCA) leads to a reduction in the distress rural out-migration (CRSR) from districts over arid and semi-arid zones of India. Furthermore, improvements in non-agricultural employment opportunities, viz., enhanced employment in factories (CADE), enhanced employment in mining and quarrying sector (CWMQ), and overall non-agricultural development (DNAD), encourage rural out-migration. In terms of factors operating in the source and destination areas, the results are quite consistent with the factors stated to be affecting rural out-migrational flows as discussed in the literature.

Similarly, we find that all the agricultural variables, viz., annual normal rainfall (DANR), irrigational intensity (CIRI), per capita foodgrain production (DFPE) and improvements therein (CFGP), forest-covered area (CFCA) have significant effects on environmental conditions, cropland areas and common land areas in expected directions. Improvements in irrigation intensity and improvements in per capita foodgrain production and forest-covered area result in improvements in environmental conditions characterised by reduction in sheep and goats as per cent of total livestock population. Furthermore, the improvements depict increase in cropland areas or net sown area, and reduction in common land areas.

The strong interconnections between the four crucial endogenous variables standing for distress rural out-migration (CRSR), the environmental degradation process as measured by changing livestock composition in terms of proportion of sheep and goats to total livestock population (CPSG), changes in land use patterns characterised by changes in net sown area (CNSA) and common land area (CCLA), are revealed through significant structural coefficients estimates of the simultaneous equations system. The multiple influences among the four endogenous variables get revealed by the structured formulations and estimated parameters of the system. The 3SLS system method of estimation provides consistent and efficient estimates of the structural coefficients. Thereby, the reduced form estimates of the system reveal that total effects of the significant exogenous variables are far more intense than their direct effects, characterised by the estimated structural coefficients.

3.6 Summary and Conclusions

Most of the interlinkages between groups of variables depicting environmental changes, population movements and redistribution process, employment structural variables depicting developmental patterns, etc., turned out to be consistent with general expectations in the factorial investigations. It may be noted here that the semi-quantitative insights, provided by the factorial investigations and theoretical and logical considerations, helped in the formulation of the structural system to quantify such structural linkages for further multivariate analysis. These insights also helped to highlight partial and total impacts of exogenous variables on the key or endogenous variables in the system. In brief, the distress rural out-migration in arid and semi-arid zones over the central and the western parts of India seems to be largely because of push factors operative at the place of origin such as environmental degradation process (CPSG) and shrinkage of common property resources (CCLA). Interestingly, we find that pull factors such as employment opportunities in non-agricultural sectors such as industrial units or mining and quarrying sectors, do not have a significant impact on rural out-migration in these regions. Thus, in a sense, the out-migration flows from rural tracts in these regions have rightly been classified as distress out-migration.

The district-level analysis reveals two concomitant processes in the arid and semi-arid regions. First, intensive cultivation on privately-owned land in these areas provides employment opportunities and thus results in in-migration to such areas within arid and semi-arid regions. Obviously, there are limits to such a pattern of intensive cultivation and thus in-migration. Second, the process of out-migration from environmentally degraded areas, primarily because of forest depletion, also gets reflected in the district-level analysis.

The simultaneous equations framework based on secondary data indicates that in the arid and semi-arid regions of India, a large part of out-migration is because of push factors such as environmental degradation and shrinkage of common property resources. The system clearly reveals that distress out-migration from rural tracts in the arid and semi-arid regions can be contained by regeneration of forests and pastureland, improving irrigational potential and bringing more land under the common property regime.

APPENDIX

TABLE A3.1
Varimax Rotated Factor Structure for District's Natural and Migrational Growth Potentials

Variable*	Factor Loadings on Variables		Communality
	I (DNGP)	II (DMGP)	
1. DPMF	0.72 (.21)	−0.30 (.11)	0.61
2. DPDA	0.74 (.21)	−0.28 (.10)	0.62
3. DCBR	0.82 (.24)	−0.06 (.02)	0.67
4. DCPR	−0.77 (.22)	0.04 (.02)	0.59
5. DDEN	−0.10 (.03)	0.59 (.22)	0.36
6. DLIT	−0.78 (.22)	0.39 (.15)	0.77
7. DURB	−0.24 (.07)	0.86 (.32)	0.79
8. DAGW	0.29 (.08)	−0.74 (.28)	0.64
9. DEFP	−0.37 (.11)	0.54 (.20)	0.43
10. DSER	−0.51 (.15)	−0.64 (.24)	0.68
Eigen Value	3.48	2.66	

* Definitional aspects of the ten variables are furnished in section 3.3.1.
1 Figures in brackets are the factor score coefficients.
  Ist Factor : Natural Growth Potential
  IInd Factor : Migrational Growth Potential

TABLE A3.2
List of Selected Variables for Factorial Investigations

No.	Abbreviated Name	Variable
Demographic		
1.	DPGS	District's Population Growth, 1971–81.
2.	DPGE	District's Population Growth, 1981–91.
3.	DNGP	District's Natural Growth Potential Index, 1981.
4.	DMGP	District's Migrational Growth Potential Index, 1981.
5.	DPDE	District's Population Density per sq. km, 1981.
6.	DENN	District's Population Density per sq. km, 1991.
7.	DSRE	District's Sex Ratio (Females per 1000 Males), 1981.
8.	DSRN	District's Sex Ratio (Females per 1000 Males), 1991.
9.	DSAE	District's Sex Ratio in Rural Areas, 1981.
10.	DSAN	District's Sex Ratio in Rural Areas, 1991.
11.	DUPE	District's per cent Urban Population, 1981.
12.	DUPN	District's per cent Urban Population, 1991.
13.	DLTE	District's Literates per 1000 Population, 1981.
14.	DLTN	District's Literates per 1000 Population, 1991.
Land Resources		
15.	DGAE	District's Geographical Area (1000 Sq. Kms), 1981.

(Contd on next page)

TABLE A3.2 (Contd.)
List of Selected Variables for Factorial Investigations

No.	Abbreviated Name	Variable
16.	DGAN	District's Geographical Area (1000 sq. kms), 1991.
17.	DNAS	District's Net Sown Area (1000 sq. kms), 1974.
18.	DNAE	District's Net Sown Area (1000 sq. kms), 1984
19.	DFAS	District's Forest Area (1000 sq. kms), 1974.
20.	DFAE	District's Forest Area (1000 sq. kms), 1991.
21.	DFDE	District's Forest Area Under Dense Cover, 1991.
22.	DFGS	District's Forest Areas per cent of Geographical Area, 1974.
23.	DFGN	District's Forest Areas per cent of Geographical Area, 1991.
24.	DFPS	District's Per Capita Food Grain Production, 1974.
25.	DFPE	District's Per Capita Food Grain Production, 1984.

Water Resources

No.	Abbreviated Name	Variable
26.	DANR	District's Annual Normal Rainfall (mms), 1974.
27.	DGIS	District's Gross Irrigated Areas as per cent of Gross Cropped Area, 1974.
28.	DGIE	District's Gross Irrigated Areas as per cent of Gross Cropped Area, 1984.

Livestock

No.	Abbreviated Name	Variable
29.	DNSS	District's Number of Sheep, 1974.
30.	DNGS	District's Number of Goats, 1974.
31.	DSGS	District's Sheep and Goats, 1974.
32.	DLCU	District's Total Livestock in Cattle Unit, 1974.
33.	DNSE	District's Number of Sheep, 1984.
34.	DNGE	District's Number of Goats, 1986.
35.	DSGE	District's Sheep and Goats, 1986.
36.	DTLE	District's Total Livestock, 1986.

Employment

No.	Abbreviated Name	Variable
37.	DAWE	District's Agricultural Workers as per cent of Total Main Workers, 1981.
38.	DAWN	District's Agricultural Workers as per cent of Total Main Workers, 1991.
39.	DWRE	District's Agricultural Workers as per cent of Main Workers in Rural Areas, 1981.
40.	DAWM	District's Agricultural Workers as per cent of Main Workers in Rural Areas, 1991.
41.	DWME	District's Workers Employed in Mining and Quarrying per Lakh Population, 1981.
42.	DWMN	District's Workers Employed in Mining and Quarrying per Lakh Population, 1991.
43.	DEFE	District's Average Daily Employment in Factories per Lakh Population, 1981.
44.	DEFN	District's Average Daily Employment in Factories per Lakh Population, 1991.

TABLE A3.3
Summary Statistics for the Selected Variables for the Factorial Investigations

Variable	Central Plateau and Hilly Region		Western Plateau and Hilly Region		Western Deserts	
	Mean	SD	Mean	SD	Mean	SD
Demographic						
1. DPGS	27.827	6.110	24.432	5.542	37.179	6.965
2. DPGE	26.703	5.654	25.727	5.699	32.24	5.864
3. DNGP	1.135	0.577	−0.265	0.893	0.907	0.323
4. DMGP	−0.578	0.599	−0.541	0.855	−0.432	0.517
5. DPNE	143.30	55.790	166.91	59.254	86.444	65.653
6. DPDN	185.93	78.766	214.03	74.002	113.00	85.846
7. DSRE	906.24	53.013	951.15	26.169	920.89	49.144
8. DSRN	897.26	49.347	945.06	21.871	913.78	46.808
9. DSAE	1031.9	803.47	963.11	27.873	930.06	46.799
10. DSAN	901.35	55.506	955.65	22.761	923.56	46.635
11. DUPE	19.314	13.683	23.497	12.727	21.046	11.253
12. DUPN	21.990	13.68	25.914	13.258	21.626	11.010
13. DLTE	26.326	6.973	37.559	11.626	20.889	6.091
14. DLTN	34.040	7.683	43.962	11.860	27.728	6.747
Land Resources						
15. DGAE	8.132	3.2779	10.193	3.573	19.511	10.71
16. DGAN	8.127	3.2709	10.190	3.582	19.526	10.717
17. DNAS	3.674	1.5311	6.594	2.853	8.900	4.695
18. DNAE	3.721	1.4907	6.221	2.349	8.222	4.298
19. DFAS	1.542	1.4493	1.563	1.456	0.134	0.98E-01
20. DFAE	1.528	1.419	1.093	1.104	.39E-01	.29E-01
21. DFDE	0.8040	1.077	0.454	0.639	.16E-02	.42E-02
22. DFGS	17.819	12.730	15.109	12.430	1.1778	1.810
23. DFGN	17.235	13.192	11.590	11.474	0.362	0.408
24. DFPS	204.19	63.055	186.06	54.170	104.22	32.050
25. DFPE	236.72	80.408	203.88	105.35	135.22	44.113
Water Resources						
26. DANR	947.04	280.59	928.62	256.42	370.11	127.30
27. DGIS	13.980	10.478	8.102	4.0346	5.355	8.147
28. DGIE	16.852	11.779	9.758	4.2921	4.544	4.838
Livestock						
29. DNSS	0.10E+06	0.17E+06	0.70520	0.88936	0.472E+06	0.18E+06
30. DNGS	0.23E+06	0.21E+06	0.20E+06	0.17E+06	0.53E+06	0.28E+06
31. DSGS	0.33E+06	0.36E+06	0.27E+06	0.17E+06	0.10E+07	0.42E+06
32. DLCU	0.10E+07	0.60E+06	0.94E+06	0.29E+06	0.14E+07	0.55E+06
33. DNSE	0.13E+06	0.23E+06	82555	0.10E+06	0.70E+06	0.40E+06
34. DNGS	0.27E+06	0.25E+06	0.26E+06	0.12E+06	0.72E+06	0.31E+06
35. DSGE	0.40E+06	0.46E+06	0.34E+06	0.21E+06	.014E+07	0.46E+06
36. DTLE	0.11E+07	0.71E+06	0.10E+06	0.31E+06	0.21E+07	0.70E+06

(Contd on next page)

TABLE A3.3 (Contd.)
Summary Statistics for the Selected Variables for the Factorial Investigations

	Central Plateau and Hilly Region		Western Plateau and Hilly Region		Western Deserts	
Variable	Mean	SD	Mean	SD	Mean	SD
Employment						
37. DAWE	72.905	12.731	74.123	11.451	69.887	9.2143
38. DAWN	72.969	12.890	72.176	13.165	69.829	10.289
39. DWRE	84.379	5.438	85.598	4.537	79.268	9.5061
40. DAWM	85.607	5.307	86.156	4.755	79.468	11.838
41. DWME	129.00	278.63	55.294	98.639	126.00	114.30
42. DWMN	129.07	273.53	62.912	79.336	56.556	88.328
43. DEFE	292.03	497.07	836.12	812.15	178.22	271.42
44. DEFN	409.91	563.64	844.38	719.72	273.56	301.87

TABLE A3.4
List of Created Variables for the Simultaneous Structural System

No.	Abbreviated Name	Variable
Demographic		
1.	DPGE	District's Population Growth, 1981–91.
2.	DNGP	District's Natural Growth Potential Index, 1981.
3.	DMGP	District's Migrational Growth Potential Index, 1981.
4.	CDEN	Change in Density.
5.	CRSR	Change in Rural Sex Ratio.
6.	CLTR	Change in Literacy Rates.
Water Resources		
7.	DANR	District's Annual Normal Rainfall, 1974.
8.	DGIS	District's Gross Irrigated Areas as per cent of Gross Cropped Area.
9.	CIRI	Change in Gross Irrigated Areas as per cent of Gross Cropped Area.
10.	CFGP	Changes in per Capita Food Grain Production.
Employment		
11.	CAWM	Change in Agricultural Workers as per cent of Total Rural Main Workers.
12.	CADE	Change in Average Daily Employment per Lakh Population.
13.	CWMQ	Change in Workers Employed in Mining and Quarrying per Lakh Population.
Livestock		
14.	CPSG	Change in Proportion of Sheep and Goats to Total Livestock.
Land		
15.	CNSA	Change in Net Sown Area to Total Geographical Area.
16.	CFCA	Change in Forest-covered Area.
17.	CCLA	Change in Common Land Area.

TABLE A3.5
Summary Statistics for the Created Variables for the Simultaneous Structural System

	Central Plateau and Hilly Region		Western Plateau and Hilly Region		Western Deserts	
Variable	Mean	SD	Mean	SD	Mean	SD
Demographic						
1. DPGE	26.703	5.654	25.727	5.699	32.247	5.864
2. DNGP	1.135	0.577	−0.265	0.893	0.907	0.323
3. DMGP	−0.578	0.599	−0.54118E-01	0.855	−0.432	0.517
4. CDEN	130.11	21.813	130.05	21.566	133.12	7.892
5. CRSR	96.977	12.785	99.242	0.949	99.301	0.438
6. CLTR	131.02	13.970	119.39	11.620	135.14	12.789
Water Resources						
7. DANR	947.04	280.59	928.62	256.42	370.11	127.31
8. DGIS	13.980	10.478	8.102	4.0346	5.355	8.147
9. CIRI	130.45	33.132	127.99	30.603	126.62	39.549
10. CFGP	119.73	31.170	115.51	68.524	134.59	38.752
Employment						
11. CAWM	101.51	2.686	100.66	2.3107	99.933	4.6301
12. CADE	215.86	209.36	124.02	53.161	308.20	226.78
13. CWMQ	258.96	854.01	145.95	57.924	52.349	41.284
Livestock						
14. CPSG	124.26	128.00	115.38	34.596	97.764	18.061
Land						
15. CNSA	120.41	28.883	129.77	40.683	155.71	60.161
16. CFCA	110.69	133.69	71.884	58.882	41.218	35.866
17. CCLA	104.21	41.446	141.07	80.10	129.32	21.789

TABLE A3.6
Summary Statistics for the Selected Variables in the Simultaneous Structural System

No. Variable	Mean	SD	C.V.*100	Skewness	Min.	Max.
Endogenous Variables						
1. CRSR	98.07	9.23	9.41	−8.80	13.30	105.70
2. CPSG	118.19	94.45	79.91	8.08	53.59	960.30
3. CNSA	99.43	9.95	10.00	−2.26	52.00	120.90
4. CCLA	120.83	6.31	49.91	1.92	29.13	412.80
Exogenous Variables						
5. DPGE	26.89	5.93	22.05	1.24	15.00	50.92
6. DNAD	−0.36	0.74	211.42	1.36	−1.50	2.24
7. DANR	881.66	310.22	35.18	0.30	164.00	1932.00

(Contd on next page)

TABLE A3.6 (Contd.)
Summary Statistics for the Selected Variables in the
Simultaneous Structural System

No.	Variable	Mean	SD	C.V.*100	Skewness	Min.	Max.
8.	CFCA	88.36	104.70	118.49	6.51	6.25	955.70
9.	CFGP	119.62	49.23	41.15	2.60	9.50	364.70
10.	CADE	190.11	177.79	93.47	3.40	21.77	1079.00
11.	CWMQ	194.89	616.05	316.24	8.79	1.44	5850.00
12.	CDEN	130.39	20.59	15.79	3.78	84.29	247.00
13.	DGIA	129.12	32.50	25.17	1.33	59.38	240.20
14.	DLTE	30.06	10.79	35.89	0.61	11.00	57.00
15.	DFGE	187.16	63.89	34.13	0.53	47.00	379.00

TABLE A3.7
Reduced Form Coefficients of the System

Item	Endogenous Variable			
	CRSR	CPSG	CNSA	CCLA
Intercept	289.9390	141.3205	87.80693	282.5741
Exogenous Variables				
DANR	−0.05588	−0.01140	0.014997	−0.05330
DFPE	−0.05080	−0.01036	0.01363	−0.04845
CIRI	−0.16256	−0.03317	0.04363	−0.15506
CFGP	−0.40372	0.08390	0.02822	−0.37630
CFCA	−0.16590	−0.03110	0.01176	−0.15679
CADE	0.00373	0.00138	0	0
CWMQ	0.00045	0.00017	0	0
DNAD	9.94214	2.02858	−2.66821	9.48282
DPGE	−0.02046	−0.00401	0.00153	−0.02045
CDEN	−0.62295	−0.12074	0.0123	−0.63073
DLTE	0.03545	0.01312	0	0

ENDNOTES

1. See Planning Commission ARPU document (1993).
2. It is to be noted that this is an independently-defined variable and not a residual.
3. The Centre for Monitoring the Indian Economy, which is listed as the source, collects data from different government sources and publishes it on a regular basis.

Chapter 4
Micro-level Initiatives in Semi-arid Zones: Emergence, Evolution and Impact

4.1 Introduction

The distinction between open access and common property resources, and the conversion of the former into categories of the latter are of the essence in determining the interrelationships between environmental degradation, poverty and underdevelopment. However, it is difficult to understand the different concepts of common property and consequently of CPR management without recourse to detailed observation and study of the distinction between it and private and state property. Further, a number of different terms have been used in the context of common property: 'common pool resources', 'common property regimes' and 'communal ownership' among others.[1] Each of these has a specific connotation which is contextual. As a consequence, the close perspective offered by micro studies is critical in determining whether a system of management involving the sharing of rights and responsibilities exists and is effective.

In this context, a distinction of some significance is that between the process leading to the creation of CPR management regimes and the impact of these regimes on improvements in indicators of environmental status. The first is a matter of organisational structure and institution creation; the second, that of the impact and effectiveness of the newly created institutions. This chapter investigates the relationship between the two, with a view to the hypothesis that institutions focusing on changes in property rights, in process of their evolution, tend to have stronger impacts on environment and on migration.

This chapter deals with both the process and the impact of institution creation. Sections 4.2. and 4.3 focus on a study of the process of institution formation taking the example of two major NGO initiatives in the district of Udaipur. In section 4.4, the impact of micro-initiatives of different kinds and with different levels of governmental support on economic, environmental and demographic variables is examined.

4.2 How Do Micro-level Initiatives Emerge: Phases in Evolution

What do outside interventions in rural areas mean or imply?

Development interventions in rural society by non-government institutions and individuals are not new in India. Even before the advent of development planning, social activists had alternative visions of a rural 'utopia' and attempted to replicate it at the micro level. Voluntarism, as understood at that time, arose out of the deeply conservative nature of feudal society existing in large parts of the country. It linked education, as understood in the formal western sense of the term, to development. The Gandhian concept of 'upliftment of all' was at the root of a large part of this movement. The resultant concept and practice extended into the fifties and sixties to form the basis of voluntarism marked by an intellectual richness and a pioneering idealism.[2] It must be said, however, that this voluntarism had a 'top-down' paternalistic aura around it. The key-words were, 'education', 'enlightenment' of the masses or sometimes, 'extension work'. It was, in a sense, easy for it to be replaced by a rural development bureaucracy, with its target-oriented planning and top-down approach. This took place and led, in turn, led to the over-emphasis on target-oriented hierarchical structures in the seventies.

A new understanding of the relevance of micro, non-governmental initiatives in the context of the management of natural resources came about in the decade of the eighties. By then, the state-led rural development bureaucracy had been transformed for the most part into a 'rent seeking' inefficient enterprise. Meanwhile, empirical evidence from across the world led to the understanding that state management of natural resources of a paternalistic nature had not been particularly successful and needed to be substituted for by participatory management arising out of a dialogue with rural societies.[3] In India, this happened simultaneously with a proliferation of NGO activity. For some time, a preoccupation with the different forms of grassroots interventions as an alternative approach to development occupied centre-stage. One fallout was an expansion in the size and scope of NGOs with elements of bureaucratisation creeping into their working. Subsequently, a part of the initial euphoria with respect to possibilities of success with natural resource management, outside of conventional government organisations, faded. A distinction now came to be made between NGOs and village-based user group associations. This phase also marked the emergence of contradictions within the internal structure of NGOs, leading to the beginning of a new phase in their evolution.

This phase in the evolution of local-level institutions seems to have been marked by the blurring of the distinction between government and non-government institutions and the emergence of the 'adaptive bureaucracy'.[4] Witness the emergence of Joint Forest Management as an accepted form of forest management by a large number of states and the emergence of innovative experiments pioneered from within government departments. Simultaneously, with expansion of individual NGOs came 'bureaucratisation' of activity within their structures. In a sense, this meant that the strengths of the two kinds of organisations could be combined in structuring of new user groups or self-help groups.[5] The sharp distinction, at times even adversarial postures implicit in the ideological debate of the eighties, was gradually dissolving into a more integrated picture as each sector seems to have acquired characteristics of the other. This happened in particular true when complementarities between governmental and non-governmental institutions were found to exist. Such complementarity is found to exist, for instance, in the case of watershed development work, with the network of government institutions having an edge in technology and NGOs being more adept at institutions, creation. Alternatively, a polarity between the two kinds of institutions arises in issue-based contexts. Witness for instance, the issues emerging in the context of the large dams debate. It can be concluded, in other words, institutional pluralism has emerged as the prevailing reality.

4.3 Organisations and Institutions

Within the existing plurality of institutions, a significant functional difference hinges around the distinction between an 'organisational' and an 'institution creating' focus. The first phase of intervention from above is usually identified with the existence of rural development organisations. Organisations are structured entities created with specific objectives and possessing a well-defined internal structure within which they choose to attain these objectives. The objectives, scope and sphere of activity may change over time but the internal structure, when juxtaposed with the situations in which the organisation is functioning, is seen as unchanging. Correspondingly, such organisations do not exhibit a consistent focus in changing modes of interrelationships between entities with which the organisation is interacting. They interact with existing legal entities in their attempt to improve individual or societal welfare. In the rural context, this implies that the organisation does not examine inter-household or intra-household dynamics in the context of resource ownership or management. Consequently, it does not attempt to alter this dynamics of social reality in manners that may supplement efficiency of resource use.

An 'institution creating' focus, on the other hand, begins with examination of rights to access, use and ownership of resources of individuals, households and other social groups. It confronts an existing set of social norms and practices, and questions whether they are appropriate in the context of efficient and sustainable resource management. If the need for new boundaries of access or norms of behaviour arises, the micro-initiative has to put these in place and the following steps[6] may be necessary:

(a) consensus building with respect to the need for a new dispensation: this is often the most difficult task. The need for such a dispensation is often traced back to the existence of 'economies of scope' or 'economies of scale'[7] which enable the introduction of a new technology,

(b) the laying down of detailed rules for working together on specific asset or income creation activities. In particular, the rules need to spell out inputs provided by groups or individuals and the returns they can expect from this provision. At this stage, technologies being used and modes of organisa-

tional responsibility for individual tasks need to be formulated carefully. This is the enterprise part of the micro-level initiative and the economics and technology aspects come in here,
(c) the putting in place of a system of responsibility for repair and maintenance of assets created and
(d) the sharing of output, its time and the manner in which it accrues need to be spelt out as well.[8]

Institutions, then, achieve or seek to achieve far more than an organisation, (which being itself a structured entity) can do. They have the potential of becoming agents of change in a more fundamental manner. By the same token, the degree of risk attached to their success is also higher. Organisations and institutions can also be distinguished between on the basis of the nature of their evolution. Steps in two alternative forms of evolution are shown schematically in Figure 4.1.

FIGURE 4.1
NGO INTERVENTION: ALTERNATIVE PROCESSES

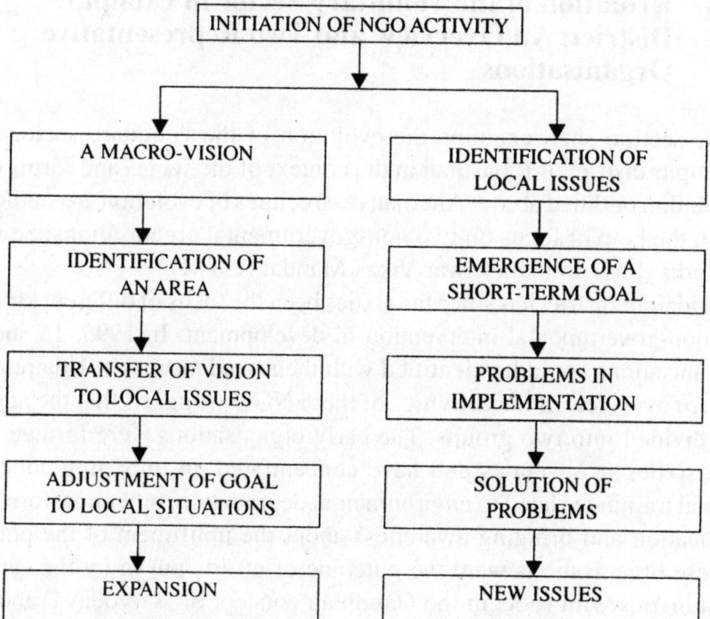

```
          INITIATION OF NGO ACTIVITY
           /                        \
  A MACRO-VISION            IDENTIFICATION OF
                            LOCAL ISSUES
         │                         │
  IDENTIFICATION OF         EMERGENCE OF A
  AN AREA                   SHORT-TERM GOAL
         │                         │
  TRANSFER OF VISION        PROBLEMS IN
  TO LOCAL ISSUES           IMPLEMENTATION
         │                         │
  ADJUSTMENT OF GOAL        SOLUTION OF
  TO LOCAL SITUATIONS       PROBLEMS
         │                         │
  EXPANSION                 NEW ISSUES
```

In the first case, the transfer of the macro vision to the area of operation and thence to issues of local significance follows. At times, the goals may be altered from the perception of the local situation. Expansion, however, takes the form of a horizontal replication of the pre-conceived macro vision. Such a model has strengths: it allows for expansion based on a conceptualisation of organisational growth. However, it is not very conducive to the creation of new institutional frameworks for rural areas, in particular, in the context of natural resource management. Another possible pitfall is the tendency towards bureaucratisation with accompanying problems.

The local issues-led intervention is more flexible in the initial stages. It draws its strength from its ability to improvise rules and conventions of behaviour. It also draws on traditional institutions to set up innovative models of management. However, expansion may bring it in conflict with other institutions that pervade the economy at the macro level. Examples are legal bottlenecks and/or market-generated constraints. The absence of a macro perspective may become a constraint at this stage in its evolution.

4.4 Evolution of the Voluntary Sector in Udaipur District: An Overview and Two Representative Organisations

This section shall examine the evolution of the voluntary sector in Udaipur district of Rajasthan in the context of the stages and forms of evolution outlined above. Alternative structures of evolution are studied with the help of focus on two non-governmental organisations: Sewa Mandir (SM) and Ubeshwar Vikas Mandal (UVM).

Udaipur district has since the sixties been the focus of different kinds of non-governmental intervention in development. In 1995, 15 such organisations could be identified with their headquarters at Udaipur.[9]

An overview of the activities of these NGOs suggests that they can be divided into two groups. The early organisations were formed in the sixties or seventies and have concentrated on imparting educational training related to environmental degradation, other non-formal education and bringing awareness about the upliftment of the poor. These organisations were the outcome of efforts put in by the early visionaries with roots in the Gandhian concept of 'sarvodaya' and a focus on rural uplift through education, health facilities and the like.

Economic opportunity was to be created through investment in social and human capital as perceived from outside the villages. Changes in income, welfare and social structure were conceived of as following in their own turn. Sewa Mandir is one of the larger organisations falling in this group. By the nineties, it had a staff of 202 and about 900 part-time members and volunteers. Furthermore, the gamut of its activities had expanded by then to include wasteland development and watershed management.

The next spurt in activity in the non-government sector in Udaipur is seen in the eighties when a large number of organisations emerged. There also emerged a new concentration on the environment. A minimum of 10 different organisations working in the area of environmental resources are located in this region. Table 4.1 lists the years of initiation of the more important ones among them.

It is found that the two phases of accelerated NGO activity were different in terms of:

TABLE 4.1
Phases in Evolution of NGO Activity: Udaipur District

Name	Year of Commencement	Staff	Part-time Member	Volunteers
I. Group 1: The early starters:				
1. Sewa Mandir	1966	202	900	4
2. Alok Nav Youvak Mandal	1969	8	17	60
3. Udaipur Environmental Group	1976	–	–	50
II. Group II: Initiatives in the eighties				
1. Sanjeev Seva Samiti	1981	8	8	10
2. The Ashoka Foundation	1982	3	–	–
3. Ubeshwar Vikas Mandal	1983	15	–	90
4. Aravali Volunteers Society, Rajasthan	1987	15	25	800
5. Adult Education Institute	1986	–	–	–
6. Bhawana Sansthan	1988	5	2	30
7. Environment Community Centre	1992	3	1	2
8. Gayatri Shiksha Sadan Sansthan	1986	16	5	50
9. Gram Vikas Samiti	1984	5	25	400
10. Gyan Bharati Trust	1985	8	–	100
11. Jagaran Jan Vikas Samiti	1985	17	30	800
12. World Wide Fund for Nature	1993	–	–	–

Source: World Wide Fund for Nature (1994).

(a) the vision or the model on which they were built up,
(b) the organisational structure characterising them and
(c) the manner in which they approached their set objectives.
NGOs formed in the eighties and nineties have had more focused programmes form the initiation itself. The stress has largely been on conservation of environment through programmes of wasteland development, water and soil conservation and the like.

Together the two organisations, Sewa Mandir and Ubeshwar Vikas Mandal, committed to the promotion of community management of eco-cultural regeneration in the rural areas of Udaipur, are fairly representative of the broad features of the NGO movement in Udaipur. Both organisations involve people at the grassroots level for the protection and management of natural resources and upliftment of their socio-economic status.

The pattern of evolution of the two is, however, different. In one case, that of Sewa Mandir, the evolution is from a broad base into areas of specific interest as found to emerge after working with the people or otherwise. In the second instance, that of Ubeshwar Vikas Mandal, the organisation begins with a focused interest on land and water management activities. Does this process of differential evolution have a bearing on their impact and on their sustainability? The following sections study the two evolutionary processes in order to investigate this issue.

4.5 Emergence and Evolution of Sewa Mandir

Conceived in 1966, Sewa Mandir was initially based on an education-oriented approach to extension work in rural areas. The area of operation of Sewa Mandir covers six blocks of Udaipur, viz., Badgaon, Gogunda, Girwa, Jhadol, Kotra and Kherwara. Since its inception, Sewa Mandir has been running various centres for imparting educational services in villages falling within these six blocks. This emphasis on education and extension is clear from publications such as the monthly newspaper called Sewa Sadhana Kranti, a monthly literary journal—Saaksharta Sandesh and a newsletter called Gati Bimal. A cultural wing called Lok Sanskriti Ikai was established to educate villagers through audio-visual shows, publication of educational bulletins in the local dialect and educational tours. The adult education wing conducted motivational campaigns and provided training in the form of formal teaching of literacy skills. Residential training is imparted by Mohan Singh Mehta Centre for Training, Kaya. It also helps various schools in exposing children to rural development activities.

Further, a People's Management School (PMS) has been set up by Sewa Mandir with the idea of providing knowledge relevant to people's lives and situations. The unit aims to *i*) develop an orientation course for Sewa Mandir workers, keeping in mind the perspectives of people-based development; *ii*) provide training material for paraprofessionals; and *iii*) educate villagers to participate in the development programmes.

Sewa Mandir also initiated a health programme in a number of villages. A number of health workers, including village health workers, traditional birth attendants, home remedy workers and pre-school nursery teachers, are trained. These village health workers promote health education, provide creative services and establish a link between their community and the existing government infrastructure for health care. Traditional birth attendants educate local women in conducting safe deliveries and immunisation of the mother and the child against diseases.

The broad-based objectives of Sewa Mandir are also clear from the following quote from Mohan Sinha Mehta, its founder:

"where there is sorrow, where there is poverty and oppression, where man is inhuman to man, it is there that Sewa Mandir must reach out, . . . Sewa Mandir is an effort to build a new social order through service, dedication and non-violent revolution" (from one of the first issues of Saaksharta Sandesh).[10]

This broad-based approach to rural development has been the characteristic feature of the organisation through the eighties and the nineties. Note, for instance, that in 1989, a Council for Advancement of Peoples' Action and Rural Technology (CAPART) supported programme on women's heath was undertaken. This provided for training inputs to traditional birth attendants. The pre-school health programme for children is also a joint project with the Women and Child Care Unit. The organisation has also received positive support from the medical department in its health programme. A government-collaborated project, called SWACH was undertaken in 1989 with a view to promote health education, specifically safe drinking water.

The emergence of environment related projects in the eighties can be said to mark a new phase in the development of this organisation. At the outset, Sewa Mandir proposed collaboration with the Centre for Developing Societies and the emphasis was on an alternative developmental model with regeneration of the environment at the centre. Simultaneous support from the National Wasteland Development Board augmented this idea. Interest in environment related development went through a series of developmental phases, somewhat in accordance with similar evolution at the national level. The three phases were: the plantation and social forestry phase, the plantation on wasteland phase, and the last phase was marked by the beginning of a group-oriented focus.

The social forestry programme of Sewa Mandir aims at alleviating economic distress of the rural people and making them self-reliant by mobilising their energies and efforts.

The main objectives of this programme are to:

  i) fulfill the fodder, fuelwood and timber requirements of the people;
 ii) provide employment opportunities;
iii) tap forestry skills of the local people;
 iv) popularise economic tree farming along with crop farming; and
  v) integrate economic gains in the distribution of benefits to the people.

The social forestry programme started with an individual beneficiary-oriented schemes and community beneficiary-oriented schemes were added later. Under the former, farm forestry, tree plantation and kisan nurseries are included. The villagers are encouraged to raise these on their own lands. Sewa Mandir supplies plants of desired species, technical know-how, seeds and insecticides free of cost to the villagers. Under the latter scheme, raising of woodlots on common grazing land called Gochar, is encouraged. For this, the villagers have to contribute on their own, though the organisation helps in protection and plantation of land and in evolving mechanisms to share the benefits from the plantation. This is done by the community asset development unit.

In 1986, Sewa Mandir started a wasteland development programme. In this programme also, initially the villagers were motivated to plant saplings on their own holdings. Later, they were encouraged to pool their privately-owned contiguous lands, called 'chaks' for collective management. The objective of restoring productivity of land was extended from 'chaks' to village common land and the revenue land. Due to low survival rate of saplings, Sewa Mandir extended support for fencing and other protective measures also. The project is continuing.

Different phases in the evolution of Sewa Mandir are implicit in the move from plantation on individual land to that on common land. 'The story of Barava'[11] illustrates this too. Note the sequence of events referred to,

"Barava's relations with Sewa Mandir date to Adult Education days. But it is only since 1987 that work began on the basis of local needs, local resources. . . it was for the first time that farmers interested in planting trees on their private land were selected and work began" and again, "within six years duration of this afforestation programme, intended to green the entire wasteland within the boundaries of their village. Of this, half of the wastelands of Barava today bear witness to the villagers commitment."

In the area of water conservation, the engineering unit of the Sewa Mandir is engaged in the construction of anicuts and completion of feeder canals. Almost all the households, where Sewa Mandir works, depend on wells and jack-wells for irrigating their lands. The organisation has helped in building lift irrigation system in a number of villages. The project in Kherwara block became operational from 1986. The machinery used for life irrigation is protected either by the villagers themselves or on a community basis.

In a sense, the evolution of Sewa Mandir from 1966 and 1996 reflects the different stages in the evolution of rural development in India. The shift of focus from educational extension to land and other asset-based interventions, the coming in of social forestry, wasteland development, soil and water conservation in the eighties and nineties all find a place in the programmes of the organisation.

This lateral movement of Sewa Mandir from one area of activity to another is facilitated by the fact that it is one of the larger NGOs in the area, perhaps the largest in terms of membership, staff and organisational structure. There are 175 full-time staff members in Sewa Mandir with approximately 700 village based para-professionals. The organisational structure at the district level is well articulated and has remained in place over a long time and provides all regulatory, technical and administrative support. It is assisted by appropriate built up at the block level. Each block, except Gogunda, is subdivided into a zonal office, headed by a block coordinator and assisted by zonal workers and para-workers. The para-workers, partly supported by Sewa Mandir, work with the villagers.

4.6 Emergence and Evolution of a Smaller Organisation: Ubeshwar Vikas Mandal

Ubeshwar Vikas Mandal, formed in 1983, is a registered, non-profit, voluntary organisation working in two hilly tribal blocks, viz., Gogunda and Bagdaunda, of Udaipur district. It is, as stated earlier, a smaller, albeit more narrowly focused group than Sewa Mandir. The name of the organisation, 'Ubeshwar', has originated from a Sanskrit word, which means 'dual divinity'. The basic philosophy behind its ideology can be stated thus: matter as well as spirit is divine and so consumption of goods should be restricted only to real need and not open to greed. This dual divinity has been the guiding principle behind the working of this organisation. The main objective of UVM is, therefore, to see that economic regeneration takes place in its physical sense. Secondly, it emphasises a simultaneous progress in educational and cultural reorientation, so that eco-regeneration is restored and protected in the future. The organisation believes in the dictum—physical improvement of man's surroundings is intrinsically related to man's own qualitative improvement.

Ubeshwar Vikas Mandal had a primary membership of 23 persons, of which 19 were adivasis. In 1989, two women social workers were added to the staff. At present, UVM has seven workers including one women worker.

The area of operation of UVM extends to nearly 28 villages. The organisation is in constant touch with each village though the number of households with whom contact exists may vary from village to village.[12] Most villagers belong to adivasis of the Bhil tribe. The main kinship groups settled in the region are Tawer and Kharadi. UVM provides financial support (wherever necessary) to the tribal community in order to establish ecological balance and enhance the productivity of their land, forest and water regimes through various programmes. Projects like pasture regeneration, wasteland development, water development/soil and water conservation, forest regeneration, and construction of wells for lift irrigation, have been initiated through organised action. The society also provides support and knowledge to the villagers on various issues pertaining to social and environmental justice. It plays a positive role in mutual aid or 'adsi padsi' effort by the people in improvement of their own assets. The community self-management or self-planned reconstruction programme carried out various activities like road construction, manure pits, drinking water troughs, land improvement, feed and breed improvement, vegetables growing, fodder storage and plantation.

The organisation has also maintained interaction with other organisations on common issues and concerns. It actively supports and participates in movements/workshops related to prevention of natural resource degradation at the national and international levels. For instance, in 1984, UVM launched 'Save Aravalli Campaign' to highlight the degradation of wasteland.

A number of organisations provide funds for meeting the expenses of the society.[13] Through various eco-restoration activities, UVM was successful in involving, organising and mobilising a large number of people in its programme of self-management in the eighties. Two indicators of success are: extent of land covered and number of households in contact with the organisation.

Under the wasteland regeneration efforts in Dhar-Badanga-Ravla-Mahua Unit, 1876 hectares of private and community pasture land was undertaken for protection, plantation, pit digging and nursery raising work from 1984 to 1989. From 1986 to 1988, 235,000 saplings in 25 nurseries, 880,000 saplings in 98 nurseries and 408,000 saplings in 81 nurseries were raised. More importantly, the villagers drew up rules and made arrangements for equal distribution of fodder from these lands. In emulation, villagers in the nearby villages also started protection work on their lands. Further, an area of 1500 hectares was taken up for survey and planning for micro-watershed regeneration. Soil and water conservation work was conducted on 1500 hectares in 12 villages. Similar achievements have been documented in the area of construction of tanks, gobar gas plants, deepening of wells for drinking water, food aid to disabled, etc., during the period from 1984 to 1989.

A new turn in the activities of the UVM came in 1991–92 when a committee for struggle against drought, led by local activists, was formed with its help in 1991–92. In this activity, the UVM was, in a sense, acting as a catalyst for initiating grassroots activity. Simultaneously, it continued its support of activities under the rural development programme.[14]

Selective spatial focus on a few villages always formed a part of activities of UVM. A rapid expansion of the society's efforts in the community self-management work was evidenced in Patia, Bagdaunda Kheda and the Dhar-Bunadia villages. While most efforts were in the area of natural resource regeneration, an expansion into areas such as promotion of non-formal education, provision of information on animal husbandry practices and introduction of social reforms like control of excessive consumption of liquor also seems to have taken place. In addition to these, the village committee monitors and ensures proper functioning of the public distribution system for essential commodities.

Ubeshwar Vikas Mandal launched a community-led irrigation project on self-help basis in Bagdaunda Kheda in 1991. Villagers dug open wells with the assistance of the society. A lift irrigation scheme was also approved by District Rural Development Agency (DRDA). In the Dhar-Bunadia belt, the construction of micro-watershed project check dam has been extended. It is also planned to construct a small anicut along the main stream. In some villages, for instance, Patia, Mokhi, Morval, Jogion ka Kheda, Vanion ka Kheda and Bagdaunda Kheda, contour bunding, check dam/field bunding, lift irrigation system, pasture regeneration and plantation have been carried out on a mutual aid basis.

The evolutional pattern of Sewa Mandir and UVM seems to suggest a dilemma which non-governmental initiatives often have to face. Once some credibility is established in a few villages, demand for involvement in wider spheres of the economic and social life of those villages emerges. Such involvement is likely to help in development of autonomous institutions within the village but requires a quantitative and qualitative strengthening in the human resources at the disposal of the organisation. There may exist constraints to this. Even when financial resources exist or can be obtained, the structure of the organisation is likely to suffer from the ills of bureaucratic lethargy and indifferent quality of some of the staff, once the initial impetus based on inspired leadership is lost. On their part, very few villages seem to reach a point where they are self-propelling in terms of institutional change to suit new situations. This demand for continued dependence on outside support seems to exist even in villages such as Sukhomajri and Ralegan Sidhi, the so-called success stories in institution creation with non-governmental support.[15] The cases studied suggest that the following sequence of events is likely to mark the emergence of the NGO form of organisation:

- the perception of a problem.
- the presence of initiative, originating almost always outside of the rural setting,
- the focusing on core areas of work, the spread to a larger and larger group of people,
- the ability to see challenges in new problems and the ability to respond to newly emerging situations outside of its area of work,
- the reaching of a plateau where a fresh spurt of initiative is needed. Ideally this should emerge from within the rural environment.

4.7 An Impact Assessment of Alternative Interventions in the Arid and Semi-arid Regions

This section assesses the impact of selected intervention on land and water management in the arid and semi-arid areas, which are defined to include the 89 districts studied in the third chapter. In selecting the projects, an effort is made to cover all agro-climatic subzones of the region. In addition, the following criteria are kept in mind:

- The experiment should have involved some change in property rights towards the direction of creation of common property. It could be a movement from government or from private ownership towards common property.
- It should have envisaged the introduction of a new technology that increased land productivity.

The focus, in other words, is on viewing these experiments as applications of technology in different agro-climatic conditions, with an attempted change in the structure of property rights.

It may be useful to add what we do not attempt to do. The impact of the newly emerging relationships on the structure of equity within the organisation are not of much interest from the viewpoint of the study. The experiment may indeed be a method of reaping the economies of scale necessary for the introduction of a new technology without much emphasis on intra-group distribution.

The projects selected for study with the help of these criteria are described briefly below.[16] The Tejpura watershed, located in district Jhansi in the central plateau has been studied as an example of technical interventions which take the form of soil and water conservation measures, afforestation, dry land horticulture and farm forestry measures. The project resulted in increased productivity and in a higher level of cropping intensity on private lands which have resulted, in turn, in higher farm incomes. This project, undertaken in 1983, had six components which were integrated to increase productivity in micro-watershed conservation with the watershed as the unit without attempting to alter the social organisation or the form that property rights took in the area.

In contrast, other experiments at the micro level included within their purview, both property rights and technical interventions. Whereever plantations on common lands have been attempted, the issue of spelling out property rights and of the organisation that accompanies such delineation becomes crucial. In this category, the Jawaja project in Ajmer district, Ubeshwar Vikas Mandal, and Ralegaon Siddhi in Ahmednagar were selected for study.

As an example of the implementation of joint forest management on forest land, the Harda project in Hoshangabad district was selected for in-depth study. On ground, user rights of people do exist within the legal framework, an increase in biotic pressure results in forest areas being treated more as open access property. In this experiment, joint forest management seeks to make de facto users partners in the process of managing forests.

Table 4.2 lists the five projects selected for in-depth study. In each case, the population, the migrational status of the district in which the project is located, the natural component index of population growth, the primary and secondary impact and the indicators of success as perceived and projected by the implementing agency are tabulated. The unit of activity, in some cases, spreads over a number of villages and/or watersheds. The Harda project, for instance, is spread over six forest ranges; 150 forest protection committees were set up in 15 villages. The Jawaja project had an area of operation of 30 villages in

TABLE 4.2
Characteristics of Selected Projects

	Projects Units	Tejpura	Harda
1. Location	District State Agro-climatic Zone	Jhansi UP 8	Hoshangabad MP 8
2. Period Undertaken		1983–85	1991
3. Unit of Work		Watershed	Forest ranges, six village forest protection committees (150 in 15 villages)
4. Nature of Work		Soil conservation, water resource development, management of crop husbandry, grass and farm forestry afforestation	Grazing control, distribution of fuel stocks, physical irrigation works, mechanism for control created, dissemination of information
5. Ownership of Land Affected (HA)		Private: 525.6 Common: 30.19	Private: 1426 Govt. forest land-10060
6. Impact of Property Rights		Marginal	Creation of rights on government-owned land
7. Population (no.)		1400	5158.00

(Contd on next page)

TABLE 4.2 (Continued)
Characteristics of Selected Projects

	Projects Units	Tejpura	Harda
8. Migrational Status of District	Nature	Immigration	Out-migration
	Index	0.41	−0.27
	Rank	97	179
9. Natural Growth Index of District	Index	0.49	0.88
	Rank	134	85
10. Primary Impact		Increase in productivity of private land 226 per cent increase in cultivated area 23.9 per cent, annual farm income increased 8.5 times	Rotational grazing accepted: 36.9 per cent closed to grazing; distribution of fuel
11. Externalities (Secondary)		Accumulation of ground water, water table increased by 3 m to 7 m in different seasons	Area increased = 31.64 per cent, soyabean introduced
12. Indications of Success		Increased income of people	Control over distribution and grazing accepted, fines imposed: 15 cases in 2 ranges, women members: 274 in 2 ranges

	Projects Units	Jawaja	Ralegaon Siddhi
1. Location	District	Ajmer and Bhilwara	Ahmednagar
	State	Rajasthan	Maharashtra
	Agro-climatic Zone	8	9

2. Period undertaken	1982 onwards	1976 onwards
3. Unit of Work	Village-30	village–1 (4 watersheds)
4. Nature of Work	Plantation on private and common land, appropriate technology for development of common lands, contour channels, trenches, check dams	Plantation on watershed, soil and water conservation, economy of fuel use, recycle of product
5. Ownership of Land Affected (HA)	Common areas – 1774 Area worked – 289 or 16.3 per cent of total common land	Wasteland: 122.71 govt. pastures: 50.78 govt. forests: 136.8 cultivable village. panchayats: 3.95
6. Impact of Property Rights	Creation of rights on common lands	Creation of rights on common lands
7. Population (no.)	9235 (in 7 villages) Ajmer Bhilwara	1508.0
8. Migrational Status of District	Nature: Immigration Out-migration Index 0.50 -.90 Rank 93 304	Out-migration -0.28 181
9. Natural Growth Index of District	Index 0.42 1.22 Rank 140 48	-0.86 301
10. Primary Impact	Average rate of survival of plantation on private and common land increased, technical interventions by way of check-dams, contour channels and trenches	Increase in productivity of private land 20–50 per cent. Increase in area cult.: 233 hc. or 37.2 per cent water conservation: 40 new wells, rise in watertable, saving in fuel consumption of 16.2 per cent due to smokeless, recycling of manure, biogas plant

(*Contd on next page*)

TABLE 4.2 (Continued)
Characteristics of Selected Projects

Projects Units	Jawaja	Ralegaon Siddhi
11. Externalities (Secondary)	Increase in productivity of crops	Augmentation of ground water, tree and grass covers
12. Indications of Success		Migration reduced to zero from 200–250 people; 13.3 per cent to 16.6 per cent of the population. Self-sufficiency in foodgrain. import of foodgrain decreased from 60 per cent to 0 stock of 150 qtls

Projects Units	UVM
1. Location	
District	Udaipur
State	Rajasthan
Agro-climatic Zone	8
2. Period Undertaken	1986
3. Unit of Work	Hamlet (part of multicaste village) selected for study
4. Nature of Work	Development of community pastures, rules for sharing responsibilities determined at outset, development of private lift irrigation and community well
5. Ownership of Land Affected (HA)	Common lands: 119 Revenue Lands: 133 Private Lands: 605 Miscellaneous: 15

6. Impact of Property Rights		Common land put under community pastures, rotational grazing: existing rights, abbreviated conflict but creation of property rights
7. Population (no.)		468 to 5000 (part of larger village)
8. Migrational Status of District	Nature Index Rank	Out-migration −0.82 288
9. Natural Growth Index of District	Index Rank	0.97 76
10. Primary Impact		Vegetation cover increased from 5 per cent in 1986 to 80 per cent in 1993 (30 per cent of trees, 50 per cent grass), fodder productivity of Rs. 90000 from pastures of 170 ha.
11. Externalities (Secondary)		Community well lift irrigation scheme initiated, reduced soil erosion, enhanced ground water recharge, well distributed perennial stream
12. Indications of Success		Initiative from villagers for expansion to newer areas.

Ajmer and Bhilwara districts but seven of these were selected for more in-depth work from 1987 onwards. In this study, 12 and six villages, respectively, from these two projects have been studied. The work in Ralegaon Sidhi was spread over four watersheds. UVM also spreads its work over two blocks and a number of villages but one tribal hamlet, for which detailed data was available, has been selected for study.

The commonality between the experiments selected is that forms of control over use of resources have been initiated and have been perceived as being successful, though to different degrees. The total impact is the combined effect of technological change and institutional arrangements for controlled use of resources.

4.8 Impact Assessment: Indicators and their Association

The focus of this part of the study is on processes incorporating economic or institutional change. Each process embodies the character of change taking place in different directions within the project area, be it a village or a set of villages. In view of this, the statistical technique used concentrates on the qualitative aspects of association, i.e., the association of attributes. Indices are built-up for the following variables: environmental improvement, migrational status, resource base, creation of property rights and emergence of participation. Projects are evaluated in terms of the association between the vector of indices so obtained.

The environmental improvement indicator is a composite index of the following:

(i) a rise in groundwater table,
(ii) an increase in survival rate of trees planted,
(iii) a decrease in illicit felling of fuelwood and cutting of fodder and
(iv) a decrease in the population of sheep and goats.

A village/watershed having show an improvement in one of these indicators is given an index 1 for environmental improvement; if it has shown improvement in two factors, then the index is given a value of 2; and if in more than two factors the index is placed at 3.

The resource base index is determined by land and livestock owned per capita. Further, land may be defined as private, government or common depending on which is relevant from the viewpoint of the nature of work on the project. Livestock is defined as the sum total of cattle, buffaloes, camels, sheep and goats in the project area.

The level of participation of the people is also measured in a qualitative sense. The contribution of village people to the cost of community asset building in a proportional sense is taken as the indicator. This contribution is, in most cases, the imputed value of labour contributed. An index of migration for each project area is constructed on the basis of district level indices, as estimated in Gulati (1992).

Table 4.3 lists the nature of association between the attributes discussed above. A decrease in out-migration is found to be associated, in a significant manner, with environmental improvement, creation of common property rights and participation. This implies that a positive change in any of these indices shall result in a decrease in out-migration Participation indices are also associated in a highly significant manner with those of environmental improvement.

Note however that indices standing for environmental improvement and creation of property rights institutions are only marginally associated. This is perhaps because some kinds of environmental improvement, such as increase in ground water levels, can be the consequence of technical interventions on private land without any change in the existing structure of property rights.

Further, the level of resource endowment, in particular, land endowment of the unit of operation is not associated significantly with the creation of property rights, migrational change or environmental improvement. In other words, the scale factor does not seem to be important in setting the process in operation. Even villages or watersheds with limited resources by way of the land at their disposal can initiate the process of institutional change. A lower resource endowment would probably mean that the income levels that can be attained as a consequence of the change are not as high as in the case of better endowed villages/watersheds.

It is possible to conclude that the nature of change introduced at the micro level is as follows: the creation of property rights, in land in particular, through assurance of certain returns (both in the present and future) leads to labour being absorbed in the augmentation of natural capital. This labour input improves the status of degraded land

TABLE 4.3
Nature of Association: Results from Village Level Study

Endowment	Creation of Property Rights	Decrease in Out-migration	Environmental Improvement	Index of Participation	Level of Resource
1. Creation of Property rights	–	–	–	–	–
2. Decrease in Out-migration	Highly Significant	–	–	–	–
3. Environmental Improvement	Significant	Highly Significant	–	–	–
4. Index of Participation	Significant	Highly Significant	Highly Significant	–	–
5. Level of Resource Endowment	Insignificant	Insignificant	Insignificant	Significant	–

Notes: Chi-Square Tests are used to determine significance.
Highly Significant: significance at 5 per cent level
Significant: significance at 10 per cent level

and increases the carrying capacity of hitherto degraded land and results in a decrease in out-migration.

To reiterate, the collation of evidence from these micro-level studies suggests that once property rights are well-defined, either in the form of ownership rights or user rights, inputs of labour for environmental protection start coming in and the out-migration process gets decelerated. A similar process is expected to emerge with respect to forest land once joint forest management takes roots. Indications to the effect are provided both in the areas included in the present study and in earlier studies too. Technological interventions can result in some kinds of environmental improvement, for instance, ground water tables were known to rise in one case. However, technological interventions alone will not be sufficient to initiate a process that has a continuous and cumulative impact on degradation in the form of management of resources such as fuelwood and fodder by the population and increase in carrying capacity of the land. It is imperative to have in place a set of well defined property rights over common resources to be augmented and improved. It is only non-governmental organisations that have shown the capability of setting off such a change.

APPENDIX

TABLE A4.1
Selected Indices for Udaipur and Rajasthan

	Year	Unit	Udaipur	Rajasthan
Relative Index of Development Area		Index	53	69
Forest Area	1991	Sq. km	17279	
	1993		3228	13099
Net Sown Area			3464.62	
Net Irrigated Area			1048.63	
NSA as percentage of NIA				
Forest Area as percentage of 1991 Reporting Area		percentage	40.57	6.41
Net Sown Area as percentage of Reporting Area			40.57	6.41
Gross Irrigated Area as percentage of Gross Cropped Area			26.83	21.3
Average Size of Holding		HA	1.75	4.34
Occupied Households		thousand	562.34	
Population		Lakhs	28.89	440.06
Males			14.70	230.43
Females			14.19	209.63
Urban			4.94	100.67
Rural			23.95	339.39
Population growth rate (per annum)		percentage	2.04	2.5
Population density (person/sq. km)		nos.	167.21	128.58
Urbanisation		percentage	17.10	22.88
Literacy			34.38	38.55
Male			49.27	54.99
Female			20.44	19.00
Urban			74.44	65.33
Rural			25.81	30.37
Workers			12.51	138.62
Main Workers			9.54	
Workers as percentage of Total Population Agriculture and Allied Activities			43.28	38.87
			70.84	70.60
Mining and Quarrying			2.2	1.03
Mfg and Non-HH Industries			5.6	5.45
HH Industries			1.62	2.00
Construction			2.21	2.42
Services			17.54	18.5

Source: Centre for Monitoring the Indian Economy, Census (1991), Forest Survey of India.

TABLE A4.2
Areas of Activity of NGOS in Udaipur

Name	Area of Activity
Adult Education Institute	Adult education, environmental education, improving village sanitation and use of alternative energy
Alok Nav Youvak Mandal	Environmental training for women, constructing anicuts, land bunding, plantation
Aravali Volunteers Society	Educate people about Rajasthan environment through camps, training on afforestation, soil and water conservation, wasteland development
Bhawana Sansthan	Promote water conservation, agro-forestry, wasteland development, soil-water conservation, encourage use of smokeless chullas and biomass
Environment Community Centre	Impart non-formal environmental education, eco-development camps for tribals, nursery raising and agro-forestry, encourage use of herbal medicines
Gayatri Shiksha Sadan Sansthan	Social forestry, wasteland development, environment education and training
Gram Vikas Samiti	Wasteland development, afforestation, improving sanitation and environmental education
Gyan Bharati Trust	Propagation of medicinal plants, educational opportunities and life support protocols
Jagaran Jan Vikas Samiti	Work for upliftment of poor, promote tree planting, agriculture. Nursery raising, community plantation, village sanitation, mud solar cookers, soil conservation
Sajeev Seva Samiti	Encourage community organisation, environmental awareness, tree plantation, wasteland development, soil and water conservation, nursery raising, biogas plants, solar cookers, training masons in building biogas plant
Sewa Mandir	Promoting local initiative in developmental issues, adult and non-formal education, development of women, health, forestry, wasteland development, soil and water conservation, agricultural extension, conservation of biodiversity.
The Ashoka Foundation	Highlighting environmental issues, providing advisory and financial support, network building and communication, consultancy services
Ubeshwar Vikas Mandal	Promote eco-cultural regeneration, upliftment of adivasis in Aravali, wasteland development, nursery raising, tree planting, soil and water conservation, micro watersheds, use of alternative sources of energy like biogas, storage of rainwater

(Contd on next page)

TABLE A4.2 (Contd.)

Name	Area of Activity
Udaipur Environmental Group	Organising eco-development camps, workshops, tree planting, organise studies in environmental conservation, publishing newsletter etc.
World Wide Fund for Nature	Promotion of nature conservation and protection through support to research, field projects, education, raise funds for conservation

Source: WWF (1994).

TABLE A4.3
Support Linkages of UVM

Agency	Year	Grant (Rs.)	Work/Programme
National Wasteland Development Board, New Delhi	1986	775200	Wasteland regeneration
	1987	3438000	Wasteland regeneration
Society for Promotion of Wasteland Development, New Delhi	1986	77000	Nursery raising
	1987	49510	Mini-watershed survey
	1988	236500	Soil and water conservation
District Rural Development Agency	1985	8140	Social forestry
	1986	156140	Social forestry
	1987	83300	Social forestry
	1988	3000	Awareness camps
Public Donations	–	102000	For food aid and fodder centres
CAPART, New Delhi	–	492412	Well deepening, tanks and soil conservation
TATA Trust, Bombay		50000	Well deepening
Nagrik Rahat Smiti New Delhi	–	8450	Well deepening
ICCO, Holland	–	337453	Soil and water conservation
Sadanad Trust		25000	Cattle camps
Coalition for Environment and Development, Finland	–	70128	Nursery raising
Environment Service Group		35000	Environment awareness campaign

Source: Unpublished documents of Ubeshwar Vikas Mandal.

TABLE A4.4
No. of Households in Contact with UVM

Village	No. of Households	Households in Contact with UVM	Percentage
Uni Phala	300	125	41.67
Kheri ka Bala	40	26	65
Nal ka Vas	46	46	100
Thoria Bhilwada	46	40	86.9
Banadia	70	70	100
Banduga	100	50	50
Rebanyon ka Kheda	32	30	93.7
Bagdaunda Gavari	27	27	100
Bama	50	30	60
Patia	263	232	88.2
Morval	150	30	20
Futiya ka Kheda	200	32	16
Kudan	100	30	30
Jeri	90	32	35.5
Bagdaunda ka Kheda	70	50	71.41
Gojaour Ka Kheda	40	20	50
Majam	200	50	25
Dhata	250	30	12
Jogion ka Kheda	50	50	100

ENDNOTES

1. See among others, Ostrom (1990) for the definitional nuances.
2. See Jones (1993) for a historical interpretation of the voluntary movement in Rajasthan in particular, which led to the foundation of institutions such as Bhartiya Vidya Bhawan and Sewa Mandir.
3. See the documentation in Berkes (1989) and Ostrom (1990) and White and Runge (1995).
4. See Haagenson (1998) and other papers presented at the Workshop on Shared Resource Management in South Asia held at Institute of Rural Management, Anand, February, 1998.
5. See Chopra (1998) for an analysis of relative strengths in the context of watershed development.
6. See Bromley (1989). For an application in the context of water user associations in India, see Kolavalli (1997).
7. See Quiggin (1993) for a distinction between the two and its implications for common property management.
8. For a study of institution building at the micro-level in Palamau, see Chopra and Kadekodi (1999). See also Kadekodi (1997).
9. See Appendix Tables A4.2 and A4.3 for a listing of names, areas of activity and year of initiation. The information is drawn from WWF (1994).

10. As quoted in Sewa Mandir Annual Report 1991-92.
11. See Madhav Tailor and M.S. Rathore in Sewa Mandir News Letter, April-June 1993 for details.
12. The reach of the society in terms of the number of households with which it is in touch in each village is given in Appendix Table A4.4.
13. Details on funding by different agencies is given in Appendix Table A4.3.
14. In 1990, the society extended its help in bunding of fields on 22 hectares in two villages, deepening of two wells, repairing of tanks, construction of check dams in eight villages, camps for environmental awareness and formation of women's savings/credit groups in five villages.
15. This observation is based on the author's field observations in each of these villages. See also Chopra, Kadekodi and Murty (1990) and Pangare and Pangare (1992).
16. These are: Tejpura watershed, a technical intervention on private land, Harda, technical-cum property rights intervention on forest land and Jawaja, Ralegaon Siddhi and UVM, interventions on village and open access land which involved both technology and property rights changes.

Chapter 5

Non-governmental Initiatives in Natural Resource Management: A Profile of Study Villages

5.1 Introduction

The concept of a village as an entity for determination of community norms and social mores has survived in Indian society despite the operation of a number of forces militating towards its weakening. It constitutes, therefore, an appropriate unit of study in the context of the impact of changing modes of natural resource management. In this chapter and the next, therefore, the village is treated as the focus in analysing the emergence and impact of natural resource managing institutions to a desegregated level. An in-depth study of six villages in the district of Udaipur constitutes the basis of the analysis.

The village community in India is at the vortex of currents of change. While maintaining its identity, it has strengthened its contacts with the city both through population movements and exposure to new kinds of goods and services. With increasing contact with village society people from cities have been exposed to the beneficial as well as detrimental changes that have been taking place in the countryside. Consequently some city-based individuals have attempted to understand and participate in the functioning of village institutions including those in the area of natural resource management. Attempts to participate in the process of modifying and reconstructing them have also emerged. The villages around Udaipur city have also experienced such interactions. Varying magnitudes of institution creation have taken place through the operation of a number of non-governmental organisations (NGOs)[1] and their interaction with the influences outlined above.

5.2 Selection of Study Villages

The selection of the six villages was made on the basis of the magnitude of institutional build-up in the form of participation in the management of common land and water resources initiated primarily by the two NGOs: Ubeshwar Vikas Mandal and Sewa Mandir. The extent of participation by the villagers has been primarily initiated and encouraged by the working of these NGOs for almost more than a decade in these villages. This was the consequence of the work done by the two NGOs, viz., Ubeshwar Vikas Mandal and Sewa Mandir, functioning from Udaipur. The work of these organisations was spread over a large number of villages. After preliminary study and participation in some village level meetings[2] organised by these NGOs, the villages were divided into the following three broad categories:

(1) those in which the NGOs had been working for more than a decade,
(2) those where institutions had been in existence for about three to five years, and
(3) those where there had been very little or almost no intervention.

The six villages selected for the detailed study are: Dhar, Gahaloton ka Vas (G.K. Vas), Patia, Bunadia, Bagdaunda and Majjam.

Two villages were selected for intensive study from each of the three categories mentioned above. The two villages, viz., Dhar and Gahaloton ka Vas (G.K. Vas), have experienced a substantial amount of intervention for more than 10 years or so. The two villages from the second category of medium-level institutional build-up are Patia and Bunadia, and the two villages with least institutional intervention and thus participation in the management of common resources are Bagdunda and Majjam.

5.3 Location of the Six Study Villages

All the six selected villages are located in the tehsils of Gogunda and Girwa of Udaipur district at distances varying between 20 to 70 kilometers from the city of Udaipur. Bagdaunda, Majjam, Patia and Bunadia are situated in the north and the northwest of Udaipur town and located in the Gogunda tehsil of Udaipur district, at a relatively greater distance compared to Dhar and Gahaloton ka Vas. The latter two villages are situated closer to Udaipur city. These two villages are located in Girwa tehsil in the upper middle valley of Ubeshwar in a watershed some 15 to 25 km from Udaipur city. The geographical locations of six selected villages and the two tehsils are indicated in the map of Udaipur district on page 106.

5.4 Inter-village Variations in the Selected Characteristics

A profile of the six selected villages in terms of different characteristics is presented in Tables. The village level information for the six study villages was elicited from village heads, teachers and government and NGO functionaries with the help of a 'village level schedule'. This region is mainly the homeland of the Bhils. The caste break-up shows that Gamatis and Meghwals constitute the majority of the households with a fair sprinkling of Gujjars, Rajputs and Brahmins in some villages. Inter-village variations in the socio-demographic characteristics are presented in Table 5.1. It is interesting to observe that variations exist in terms of population size, age structure, religious and ethnic composition of the populations, extent of accessibility to various amenities like health, education, transportation and connectivity through all-weather road or bus. Sources of livelihood from land, livestock, or casual labour, ownership of land and water resources, land use and cropping patterns, and existence of environmental upgradation programmes are discussed in the following sections.

5.4.1. Socio-demographic Profiles of the Study Villages

The number of households per village varies from a minimum of 55 households in Gahaloton ka Vas to almost 200 households in Majjam

MAP 5.1
UDAIPUR DISTRICT AND TEHSILS GOGUNDA AND GIRWA

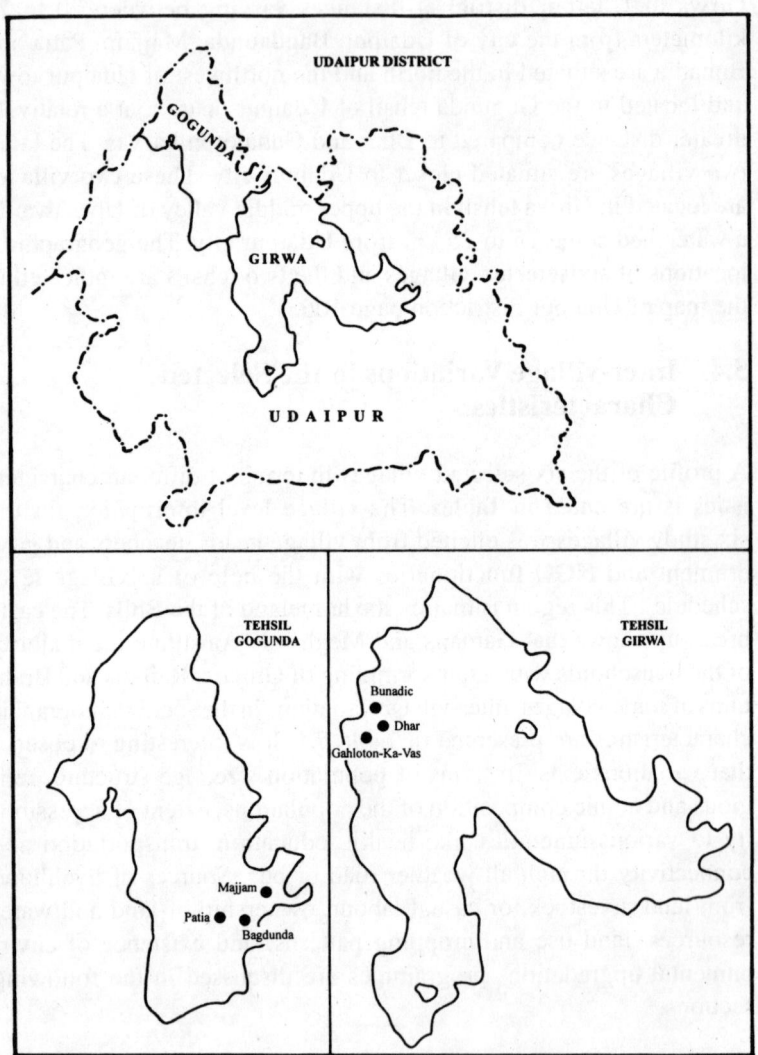

and to a maximum of 263 households in Patia village. Furthermore, the size of the population varies between a minimum of 300 in Gahaloton ka Vas to around 1500 in Patia and furthermore, to a maximum of almost 2000 in Majjam. Average household size varies and the population data reveals that Dhar, Bagdaunda and Bunadia are much smaller villages comprising only 50 to 75 households, whereas Patia and Majjam are bigger with populations of 1500 to 2000 divided into 200 to 260 households.

TABLE 5.1
Socio-demographic Characteristics in the Study Villages

Population's Characteristics	Name of the Village					
	Dhar	G.K. Vas	Patia	Bunadia	Bagdaunda	Majjam
Household Characteristics:						
Number of Households	116	55	263	70	75	200
Total Population	800	300	1500	1000	1800	2000
Number of Adults	500	105	800	261	800	550
Number of Children	300	195	700	739	1000	1450
Religious Composition:						
Hindus	All	All	All	All	All	All
Jains	–	–	–	5	–	–
Caste Composition:						
Gamatis (ST)	25	25	225	50	10	80
Meghwals (SC)	15	7	10	10	40	22
Gujjars	2	–	25	–	–	40
Rajputs	–	2	–	10	20	32
Brahmins	20	–	–	–	–	–

Note: Caste data could not be recorded for all households, hence the small discrepancies in the totals in the above table.

5.4.2. Health, Education and Community Infrastructure

Health infrastructure is inadequate and almost negligible in all the six study villages. No hospitals, primary health centres or sub-centres are found to function in the study villages. Furthermore, health functionaries of the primary health care system rarely visit the villages. Traditional medical practitioners are the only source of treatment for day to day ailments. For health problems of a more serious nature, people have to travel to the nearest town. The nearest medical store, except for Majjam where it is within 5 km, is at a distance of 15 to

25 km in all the rest of the five villages. The low level of health infrastructure is reflected in the immunisation levels of the children. Only nine per cent of the children are fully immunized against DPT, 12 per cent against polio and 17 per cent against BCG.

All villages, excepting Gahaloton ka Vas (G.K. Vas), have primary schools, with Bagdaunda having a higher secondary school. However, it is to be noted that most teachers at the time of the survey were men, except in Bagdaunda, where two women teachers were employed, one in the primary and the other in the higher secondary school. This may have some implications for the access of female children to education in the socio-cultural milieu of that region, where sending girl children to study in a distant school or in a school with only men teachers is not favoured. The average level of literacy is about 1.48 years of school. However, all children are found to be sent to primary school now.

TABLE 5.2
Health, Education and Community Infrastructure in the Six Villages

Infrastructural Facility	Name of the Village					
	Dhar	G.K. Vas	Patia	Bunadia	Bagdunda	Majjam
Educational:						
Number of Schools	1	–	1	1	2	1
Primary	1	–	1	1	1	1
Middle	–	–	–	–	–	–
Sr. Secondary	–	–	–	–	1	–
Number of Male Teachers						
Primary	1	–	1	2	2	1
Middle	–	–	–	–	–	–
Sr. Secondary	–	–	–	–	12	–
Number of Female Teachers						
Primary	–	–	–	–	2	–
Middle	–	–	–	–	–	–
Sr. Secondary	–	–	–	–	2	–
Health:						
Number of Traditional Vaids	–	2	2	1	–	–
Distance From Nearest Medical Store	20	25	15	20	10	5
Community Structures:						
Temple	Yes	Yes	Yes	Yes	Yes	Yes
Chopal	No	Yes	Yes	No	Yes	No
Panchayat Ghar	Yes	Yes	Yes	No	No	No

It is interesting to observe that all the villages have a temple where the villagers can go to perform their religious rituals and rites, whereas community meeting places or gatherings popularly known as Chopals are available only in three villages, viz., Gahaloton ka Vas, Patia and Bagdaunda. Panchayat Ghars are available again only in three villages, viz., Dhar, Gahaloton ka Vas and Patia. Interestingly, the availability of Panchayat Ghars in villages where institutional build up is maximum could also be interpreted as, in the villages where NGOs have been working for long, they have been able to impress upon villagers to invest in Panchayat Ghars.

5.4.3. Access to Infrastructural Facilities

A perusal of Table 5.3 reveals that Dhar and Gahaloton ka Vas are villages located within 20 to 25 km distance from the nearest town which, of course, is the city of Udaipur. The other four villages are located further away from the city. Though all villages are connected by 'Kucha' or unmetalled road, it becomes impossible for commuters to commute because of the difficult terrain. Furthermore, of the six villages, only three, i.e., Dhar, Bagdaunda and Majjam are connected by an all-weather road and hence by bus. Thus it is quite expected that the labourers commuting daily for employment purposes are mainly from these three villages.

TABLE 5.3
Access to Infrastructural Amenities in the Six Study Villages

Amenity and Accessibility Criterion	Name of the Village					
	Dhar	G.K. Vas	Bagdaunda	Bunadia	Patia	Majjam
Distance from Nearest Market	20	5	15	20	10	5
Distance from Nearest Town	20	25	50	70	45	60
Distance from Nearest Rly Stn	20	25	50	70	45	60
Connected by Bus	Yes	No	No	No	Yes	Yes
Connected by All-weather Road	Yes	No	No	No	Yes	Yes
Connected by Kucha Road	Yes	Yes	Yes	Yes	Yes	Yes

5.4.4. Land Ownership and Use Patterns

Livelihoods in this region depend mainly on land and livestock with casual and regular labour on nearby construction and other works, forming an important supplementary source of income. With respect to property rights, a clear perception seems to exist with regard to the difference between private land including private pasture ('beeda'), community pasture ('charnot') and forest land ('junglat'). This interestingly exhibits the difference in perception with respect to property rights at the village level as compared to that in secondary data collecting agencies. Private land ownership is widespread, with 166 of the 186 households (or about 87 per cent) owning some land. Average agricultural land owned 'however' exhibits variation from 2.87 bighas in Bagdaunda to 6.47 bighas in Bunadia.

TABLE 5.4
Land Ownership and Use Patterns in the Study Villages

Land's Ownership and Use	Name of the Village					
	Dhar	G.K. Vas	Patia	Bunadia	Bagdaunda	Majjam
Privately Owned:						
1. Total Privately-owned Land	400	300	1000	1000	200	800
A. Irrigated Land	25	25	50	20	20	50
B. Unirrigated	175	20	70	40	70	50
C. Unarable	200	250	800	800	100	700
2. Private Land Used as Common Land[3]	Not Aware	Not Aware	No	No	No	No
3. Total Common/ Panchayat Land	450	250	650	–	50	275
4. Total Forest Land	55	150	1000	–	200	500
5. Total Govt Revenue Land	50	60	300	200	20	800

Access to forest land for grazing exists, as in many parts of India. Dhar and Bagdaunda residents mentioned this access, both for grazing and for fuelwood collection. In fact these two seem to be the major uses to which forest land is put to by villagers of this region. It was stated often that forests are too degraded for medicinal plants to grow.

Gum is sometimes extracted. Fuelwood, on the other hand, is collected by 124 of the 186 households surveyed in the six villages. Further, 174 of the 186 households use wood as a source of fuel. Leaves and small timber are insignificant in comparison.

Dependence on land seems to follow the traditional pattern in which each family has some land in the low-lying areas which is cultivated or kept as private pasture. Beyond these, usually in the uplands, are the common pastures and, at a higher elevation, the forests extending up to the ridge boundaries common to other villages. This is the clearly defined eco-niche of each community, sometimes in one watershed but at others, as part of a larger watershed with numerous tributaries flowing down the Aravallis.

5.4.5. Sources and Ownership Pattern of Water Resources

Water, in general, is a scarce natural resource in this region, viz., arid and semi-arid zones in western parts of India, especially Rajasthan. The ownership and use patterns of water resources like wells, tanks and underground water in the six study villages are discussed in the following sections.

Sources of drinking water are extremely important for the basic survival of human beings as well as cattlestock in these villages. Furthermore, availability of potable water has its own special significance as water-borne diseases take a heavy toll of human life in the Indian context and especially, in this region. Droughts are quite common in these regions and thus management of scarce water resources assumes special significance.

Tanks exist in all six villages and are used for both irrigation and drinking water extraction. Like anicuts, they are both privately-owned and commonly-owned. Government-owned tanks are found only in Bunadia. Privately-owned bawaris and/or wells on the other hand, exist in all villages. The number of wells seems smaller in Dhar, Bunadia and Majjam. However, here they are supplemented by hand pumps. Tapped supply of drinking water exists only in Gahaloton ka Vas.

Table 5.5 gives the sources of water and, additionally, of drinking water. Private wells and tanks predominate. It is important to point out that some wells are clearly earmarked to be used only for drinking water. There may simultaneously exist other wells and tanks used

TABLE 5.5
Drinking Water Resources

Source of Drinking Water	Name of the Village					
	Dhar	G.K. Vas	Patia	Bunadia	Bagdaunda	Majjam
Source	Well	Well	Well	Tank	Well	Well
Number of Wells	4	20	35	3	20	2
Ownership of the Sources of Water:						
Private Wells	3	15	35	3	20	2
Taps	–	1	–	–	–	–
Hand Pumps	–	–	3	5	1	2
Tanks (Private)	1	2	2	–	2	–
Tanks (Govt.)	–	–	–	2	–	–
Anicuts	3	–	1	3	2	–

for drinking, irrigation, livestock and other purposes. At the village level, these distinctions are clearly identifiable and reflect the qualitative dimensions of water supply in a sharp manner.

Water is scarce in this region though the extent varies as between villages. Seasonal irrigation from rivers is available in all villages. A number of other sources of irrigation such as tanks anicuts, tubewells, dugwells and bawaris also exist with both community and private ownership existing.

The ownership patterns of different sources of irrigation in the villages is depicted in Table 5.7. We find that private ownership of tanks used for irrigation purposes is distributed evenly over all villages. Two privately-owned tanks exist in Dhar which has more than 10 years of NGO-initiated social interventions. Similarly, two private tanks exist in Patia which has 3–5 years of institutional build-up, and again,

TABLE 5.6
Nature of Irrigation from Seasonal Streams

Source of Irrigation	Name of the Village					
	Dhar	G.K. Vas	Bagdaunda	Bunadia	Patia	Majjam
River	Yes	Yes	Yes	Yes	Yes	Yes
Seasonal	Yes	Yes	Yes	Yes	Yes	Yes
Perennial	No	No	No	No	No	No
Availability of Seasonal Irrigation (in months)	5–6	3–4	5–6	3–4	4	4

TABLE 5.7
Ownership Pattern of Sources of Irrigation

Nature of Ownership of Sources of Irrigation	Name of the Village					
	Dhar	G.K. Vas	Patia	Bunadia	Bagdaunda	Majjam
Private Ownership:						
Tanks (Used for irrigation)	2	–	2	–	2	–
Anicuts (used for irrigation)	1	2	–	3	–	–
Tubewells	–	1	–	–	–	–
Bawaris	2	2	–	1	–	3
Dugwells	–	2	–	–	–	–
Nalas	1	–	–	–	–	–
Common Ownership:						
Tanks	–	–	3	–	2	2
Anicuts	3	–	–	–	1	–
Nalas	–	–	–	–	1	–
Government Ownership:						
Tanks	–	–	–	2	–	–

Note: The structures mentioned in Table 5.7 are those that are used for irrigation. They may or may not be used as sources of drinking water.

two tanks in Bagdaunda which does not have any or just marginal social organizational build up by the NGOs. Furthermore, we find that both in Bagdaunda and Majjam, which have minimum institutional build-up, there are two tanks each under common ownership of the villagers. Bagdaunda is the only village which has one 'nala' under common ownership of the villagers. Government-built tanks are found only in Bunadia which, of course, has experienced social organisation efforts of NGOs only since 3–5 years.

Groundwater is of good quality, locally known as 'sweet', in all the six study villages. Interestingly, an increase in the ground water table over the last five years was reported in the four study villages, viz., Dhar, Patia, Bagdaunda and Majjam. A perception seems to exist that a rise in the ground water table is due, in part, to watershed developmental activities such as field bundings, construction of check dams, anicuts and also, forest plantations. During discussions in the course of the field work, it was stated clearly that upto 1988, wells did not provide water even for animals. However, despite these changes in

TABLE 5.8
Groundwater Utilisation and its Characteristics

Groundwater Characteristics	Name of the Village					
	Dhar	G.K. Vas	Patia	Bunadia	Bagdaunda	Majjam
Is Used for Irrigation	Yes	Yes	Yes	Yes	No	Yes
Depth to Ground Water (In Feet):						
In Summer	30	50	30	60	60	40
After Rains	20	20	20	20	30	15
Has Level Changed Over Last 5 Yrs	Yes	No	Yes	No	Yes	Yes
Has it Gone Up	Yes	No	Yes	No	Yes	Yes

the underground water table, it was reported that the scarcity of water for irrigation purposes still exists and the irrigated land area is not more than 8 to 10 per cent of the total privately-owned arable land.

5.4.6. Cropping Pattern

Wheat, mustard and gram dominate the cropping pattern on privately-owned land in the rabi season and by maize, bajra and jowar in the kharif season. This kind of crop rotation is usually found in the arid and semi-arid parts of northern and western India. Further, wheat is normally grown on better quality, irrigated land. Interestingly, we find that rice is also grown in Bunadia where it has three anicuts that are privately-owned and the only village where two tanks are built up under the ownership of the government. Ginger or 'adarak' is also reported to be grown in Gahaloton ka Vas in the kharif season. However, the predominant crop during the rabi season turns out to be wheat, mustard and gram and during the kharif season, the predominant ones in the study villages are maize, bajra and jowar.

5.4.7. Ownership Pattern of Cattle Stock

Ownership of assets such as cattle is widespread in these villages. The ownership of milch animals like cows, buffaloes, goats and sheeps and drought animals like camels and bullocks seems to be quite widespread in all the study villages. Villages do not seem to differ

TABLE 5.9
Cropping Pattern in the Study Villages

Name and Type of Crop	Name of the Village					
	Dhar	G.K. Vas	Patia	Bunadia	Bagdaunda	Majjam
Rabi Crops:						
Ist	Wheat	Wheat	Wheat	Wheat	Wheat	Wheat
IInd	Sarso	Sarso	Chana	Chana	Chana	Jvar
IIIrd	Chana	Chana	Sarso	Sarso	Sarso	Sarso
IVth	–	Jvar	Rajoka	Jvar	–	Urad
Kharif Crops:						
Ist	Maize	Maize	Maize	Maize	Maize	Maize
IInd	Bajra	Adarak	Bajra	Rice	–	Bajra
IIIrd	–	Jvar	Jvar	Mung	–	–

much in terms of average level of ownership of cattle, which is between one or two standard units per household across all the villages.

We find that in villages like Patia, Bundia, Bagdaunda and Majjam, the caste of 'Gamatis' seems to have maximum concentration of cattle ownership of milch animals like cows and buffaloes. Furthermore, the concentration of goat ownership is also found to be higher in these villages. It may be of interest to mention that average milch yield from cows which are sent out for grazing, is also very low, ranging between one to two litres only. Stall-fed animals show higher levels of milk yield.

The ownership pattern of draught animals seems to be dominated by bullocks. However, the concentration of bullocks also turns out to be higher in three villages, viz., Patia, Bagdaunda and Majjam. Gahaloton ka Vas has the minimum number of cattlestock of all kinds,

TABLE 5.10
Livestock Population in the Study Villages

Category of Livestock	Name of the Village					
	Dhar	G.K. Vas	Patia	Bunadia	Bagdaunda	Majjam
Cows	100	30	150	225	200	150
Buffaloes	70	40	200	80	250	200
Bullocks	70	40	200	80	250	200
Camels	–	–	3	–	5	–
Goats	250	15	100	350	400	500
Sheeps	50	–	–	–	–	20

whether of milch or of drought category. However, the village also seems to be the most thinly-populated out of all the study villages.

5.4.8. Quality, Utilisation and Upgradation of Forest Land

Forest land is found predominantly in Patia and Majjam villages where land under forest cover is 1000 and 500 bighas respectively. In the other three study villages, we find the land under forest range just between 55 to 200 bighas. Bunadia is the only village where there is absolutely no forest area. A general perception amongst people about forest cover was reported to be that 30 to 40 years back, there used to be a lot of greenery and tall trees and bushes in the surrounding hills. They now find that these hilltops have got denuded, basically, because of felling of trees for commercial timber purposes in the adjoining city of Udaipur. Opinions were also expressed that development of Udaipur and fuelwood consumption by the city-dwellers has been responsible for deforestation and denuded hilltops.

Probing further into the improvement in the biological quality of forests, especially after the social organisation work started by the NGOs, revealed that a substantial improvement has been observed over the last ten years. The maximum improvement in the biological quality of forest was reported in Dhar village. Improvements in the villages where maximum land was under forests (viz., Patia and Majjam) were also reported to be substantial. Majjam was reported to have good natural forests over almost 60 per cent of its forest area. Furthermore, the institutional build-up in villages like Dhar and Gahaloton ka Vas has also resulted in substantial improvements in the biological quality of forest areas. Rather, percentage of land categorised under degraded forests also turned out to be minimum in Dhar village where accessibility of villagers for grazing of their animals and fuelwood collection was extended to around three months in a year on permanent basis. Thus there seems to exist some evidence that social organisational work for more than 10 years in villages like Dhar has not only improved the biological quality of forest covers but also provided better use of forests for grazing of animals and fuelwood collection to the villagers.

TABLE 5.11
Quality and Utilisation of Forest Land

Forest Land's Quality and Utilisation	Name of the Village					
	Dhar	G.K. Vas	Patia	Bunadia	Bagdaunda	Majjam
Total Forest Land (Bighas)	55	150	1000	–	200	500
Improvement in the Biological Quality of Forest Land:						
Per cent Forest Area Improving Over last 10 Yrs	50	10	10	–	10	10
Nature of Forest Plantation (Per cent Area)						
Good Natural Forest	30	30	–	–	–	60
Degraded Forest	50	80	80	–	80–85	90
Planted Forest	10	25	–	–	25	45
Accessibility of Forest Land to Villagers (In Months):						
Permanently for Grazing	3	–	–	–	3	–
Permanently for Fuelwood Collection	3	–	–	–	–	–
Periodically for Grazing	–	–	–	–	–	2

5.4.9. Migrational Patterns in the Study Villages

In addition to income from land and livestock ownership, a considerable amount of income in these villages accrues from casual labour, village industry and trading. Again, average levels differed considerably across villages, with Majjam and Gaholoton ka Vas having about half the level of income from these sources than the three villages of Bagdaunda, Bunadia and Patia. Dhar falls somewhere in between with an income of about Rs.1078 per month.

Out-migration from the villages is significant[4] with 44 out of 186 households surveyed, or about 25 per cent, reporting migration. With the total number of out-migrants being 56, the general pattern seems to be of one member from each household migrating. The distribution of this out-migration across villages is uneven, with the most accessible villages showing the lowest levels of migration. This seemed counter-intuitive and we tried to investigate whether this was because daily commutation had taken the place of permanent migration.

Daily commutation is significant with about 220 adults out of a total population of 900 odd commuting to neighbouring towns for work. The maximum number of commuters is from villages that are connected by bus. It is not distance but accessibility in terms of time spent in commuting that seems to determine its magnitude, other things being the same. Further, it is interesting to note that the extent of commuting decreases in drought years. It was stated in the course of field investigation that this was because of the start of relief works near the villages. This intervention did away with the need for commuting or migrating.

The migration is predominantly male migration, with 99 per cent of the migrants being male. Further, 42 of 44 migrants cited 'work' as the reason for migration, with only two stating that they migrated for study. Average age of out-migrants, which was about 25 years confirmed this. Occupation of out-migrants also turned out to be service and labour. Remuneration of the out-migrants showed a considerable degree of variation, from Rs. 300 to Rs. 12000 per month, with the average being about Rs. 1545.22.

The pattern of migration is also revealing. About 67 per cent of the total migration seems to have taken place in 1989 the year in or following the drought of 1988–89. This confirms the hypothesis that a large part of migration is indeed stress and not developmental migration.

5.5 Concluding Remarks

This chapter gives an overview of villages selected for an in-depth study in Udaipur district. Inter-village differences are distinct in the context of environmental variables such as depth to ground water table and the extent of improvement in forest cover over the last ten years or so. Villages also differ with respect to magnitude of out-migration as well as daily commutation. In relation to resource base such as magnitude of land or livestock ownership and quality of resources owned, there seems to be a marked similarity. The similarity, with minor variation, extends to other areas such as health and other infrastructure. Since the villages were selected in a manner so as to represent alternative levels of institution creation, the question that arises is: Is the creation of property rights emerging from the existence of NGO intervention linked to the differences observed in migration and environment related variables? This is the issue addressed in the next chapter, the analysis being based on a household survey in the six villages being studied.

ENDNOTES

1. For details, see chapter 4.
2. The village-level field study was conducted in 1995. Data tabulated in Tables 5.1 to 5.11 is from the village and household schedules canvassed in that year.
3. Conventions may exist to this effect for fallow land or for unarable land. However, information was not readily available on this.
4. Data on migration and commutation was not collected at the village level. The analysis in this section is based on information collected from the sample households.

Chapter 6

Participation, Common Property Institutions and Migration: An Econometric Exploration

6.1 Introduction

This chapter tests hypotheses relating to the impact of alternative levels and modes of institution creation with the help of econometric techniques and the household and village-level data described at length in the fifth chapter. After a brief description of the historical evolution of institution-creating activity in the six villages studied in section 6.2, section 6.3 gives details of the methodology and qualitative and quantitative variables used in the analysis. Section 6.4 analyses factors determining household decisions to migrate and/or to opt for daily commutation from the workplace in the city. Section 6.5 studies factors determining household decisions to participate in land and water-related common property management. It also quantifies magnitudes of participation and examines what factors play a role in its determination. Up to this point, the analysis is carried out in a single equation framework, either Ordinary Least Scar (OLS) or logit. Section 6.6 sets up a simultaneous structural system to model the joint determination of household decisions to migrate and/or to participate in strengthening of natural resource management in the presence of different levels of outside intervention. Finally, section 6.7 summarises the results and assesses the usefulness of econometric techniques in the above context.

6.2 Institutional Innovation, and its Evolution in the Villages

The six villages selected for study and their socio-economic profile have been described at length in the fifth chapter. These villages have witnessed a considerable degree of institutional innovation in the past decade or so. An institution in this context is a codified set of rules which, by convention or by law, mediates the nature of the relationship between people and resources. It specifies the structure within which economic transactions take place in the short run and resource management takes place in the medium and long runs. The form of an institution may need to change with time as the transaction costs associated with keeping it alive increase. This calls for institutional innovation. Institutional innovation can be visualised as a process that replaces the earlier structures with newer, more efficient ones. It is a dynamic process in which the interface of the society with the rest of the world plays an important role. Innovatory institutions emerge either as a consequence of evolution from within the community/society or with a degree of imposition from outside.

Specific tasks (as stated earlier) that the new institutions for natural resource management in each of these villages have addressed are:

(a) finding a method of rationing scarce resources in situations where the nature of the good pre-empts the existence of a market,
(b) building a system of inter-temporal allocation that overrides possible preferences of individuals for the present, and
(c) ensuring sustainable use of the resources.

Intervention in eco-restoration in the first village selected for study was made in the form of the protection of a 20-hectare private pasture area in the Dhar region for natural regeneration. This was in 1985 and even with the scanty rainfall that year, it was successful and was able to meet the community's needs for a considerable part of the year. The following year saw the expansion of activity to 600 hectares, and also saw the forest department's active involvement in it. This was followed by the initiation of planning on a watershed ecosystem basis. A micro watershed regeneration project was extended to the four revenue villages in the area. It included soil and water conservation, improved animal husbandry and agricultural practices.

In the village of Bagdaunda, the social organisation process started with,

(*a*) the setting up of a large community-based pasture in 1986 and an open well-based lift irrigation facility in 1990,
(*b*) mutual aid in labour for land improvement, and
(*c*) a women's saving group for self-help.

Initial interest in Kheda, a hamlet to the east of Bagdaunda was in pasture protection. Here, the panchayat was made partly responsible for protection with the help of a locally-appointed guard and village contribution for the salary of the guard. Later, the sustenance of interest once again centred around the community well lift irrigation scheme. Work could be started only after some conflict between two groups was resolved in 1990. Free contributory labour was made available for this well. Autonomy of judgement, action and resources was the hallmark of the process by which this was made operational.[1] In the Bagdaunda Kheda area, the social organisation geared to the two tasks of pasture protection and irrigation development has been a story of the successful interaction of the village community, the voluntary agency and the government.

Patia has seen another kind of cooperation. Here the focal point has been field bunding and cooperative work on private land. As early as 1989, the village residents have been working on the protection of each other's private land, treating it as an extension of a traditional institution called 'adsi-padsi'.

It is seen, therefore, that the process of institution creation followed different routes in each village. The starting point was either protection of a private pasture or a common pasture or the building of a common irrigation source or just the initiation of self-help groups. It was necessary to have a technically sound plan in each case and to enthuse the village residents through the establishment of links with traditionally existing institutions.

6.3 The Impact of Institutional Innovation: Variables and Methodology

This chapter aims at studying the impact of the changes outlined in section 6.2. The data base for this part of the study was generated from a field survey conducted in the selected villages in February and March 1995. Two schedules, the village-level schedule and the household-level schedule were canvassed in the six villages selected. The villages were selected so as to represent different levels of institutional intervention. As stated in the fifth chapter, levels of institution creation are distinguished between in the following manner:

(a) the reference villages were those in which no institution creation had been attempted at all, where, as was often stated by the NGOs, 'work had just been initiated'. These were Majjam and Bagdaunda,[2]
(b) villages in which some work on creation of institutions had existed for some time: these were Bunadia and Patia, and
(c) the villages of Dhar and Gahaloton ka Vas which had seen extensive involvement of two well-established institutions (UVM and Sewa Mandir for the past decade or more).

The methodology followed to test the hypothesis stated above consists of formulation of multiple regression specifications and simultaneous structural systems and thereby, estimating the parameters by both single equation and systems methods. Further, depending on the nature of the question being asked on specific response variables, a mixture of OLS and logit regression-based estimation techniques are utilised. The migration-related variables are analysed using OLS and the institutional participation using logit methods.

The time series effect of being at different stages in the process of creation of common property rights is captured through the use of dummy variables in the form of intercept dummies. This procedure was adopted to reflect, in the behaviour pattern of individuals, those aspects of institution creation that changed the nature of the village environment in which they took decisions regarding migration and participation.

At a later stage in the analysis, slope dummies corresponding to specific explanatory variables were also introduced in order to simulate the time series effect of those village level changes that affect individual behaviour through an impact on the respective slopes.

The econometric base of the study comprises of cross-sectional survey-based data from 186 households and six tribal villages. This database facilitated generation of the following two sets of variables at household and village level respectively.

6.3.1 Household Level Variables

A. *Migration Related:*
HMIG : Ratio of migrants to household members above the age of 14
HCOM : Ratio of commuters to household members above the age of 14
HREM : Remuneration per household migrating to urban areas
HRPM : Remuneration sent per month to household in village

B. *Asset and Income Related:*
HALO : Private agricultural land owned
HSCU : Standard cattle units owned[3]
HFMI : Family income from sources other than agriculture
HTCA : Total cultivable land owned
HPII : Private investment in irrigation
HPAI : Privately-owned irrigated land
HSFI : Household stall-feeding level
HCGC : Number of days

C. *Variables Relating to Institution Creation*
HPWI : A household's decision on whether or not to participate in water-related institutions (has a yes/no value).
HPLI : A household's decision on whether or not to participate in land related institutions (has a yes/no value).
HLDW : Number of days spent by households (paid and unpaid) in working on water-related institutions
HLDL : Number of days spent by households (paid and unpaid) in working on land-related institutions
SFIP : Stall-fed fodder used by the household: an indirect indicator of participation in institution creation by following norms laid down

6.3.2 Village-level Variables

A: Asset and infrastructure related
VLCL : Village specific common land
VLFL : Village specific forest land
VDTC : Distance of village from city
VWCB : Whether or not village is connected by bus
VWCR : Whether or not village is connected by road
VASF : Availability or otherwise of school in village

The logit regression technique is used to analyse the categorical variables, HPWI and HPLI relating to house decisions to participate in institution strengthening. This methodology facilitates the eliciting of effects of several predictor variables, which may be quantitative, categorical or mixture of the two, on the dichotomous response variable which depicts decisions like participation or non-participation in any collective action or basically yes/no kind of decisions on the part of the respondents.

A brief presentation of the functional form of the logit model for the present study follows. The basic form of the multivariate logistic function with Z as the predictor variable, which itself is a combination of several predictor variables (Xk's) as

$$Z = b0 \times b1 \times X1 + b2 \times X2 + ... + Bk \times Xk \qquad (1)$$

and thus the functional form of the model becomes

$$P = 1/(1+\exp(-(b0+Sbi \times Xi))) \qquad (2)$$

or alternatively the logit form of the model as follows:

$$\log W = Z \qquad (3)$$

where the odds of participation (W) becomes

$$W = P/(1-P) \qquad (4)$$

in which P is the probability of participation in any collective action or commons such as common land resources (EPCLR) or common water resources (EPCWR) in the present study and thus W depicts odds of the participation. Obviously, the reference category in the present model is no-participation in the commons and thus P provides the probability of participation in the commons.

The Maximum Likelihood (ML) estimation procedure is adopted for eliciting parametric estimates of the structural coefficients (bj's) of the model. Rutherford and Minja[4] provide detailed exposition of mathematical details of the ML estimation procedure, cautious interpretation of the estimated parameters, multiple classification analysis (MCA) based on the elicited parametric estimates, etc., in the logit regression analytical technique. The estimated structural coefficients (Bj's) estimated by the Maximum Likelihood estimation procedure and their mean values are in turn utilised to elicit the estimates of probabilities of participation or non-participation in the commons as follows.

$$Z = \exp(b0 + Sb_j \times X_j) \qquad (5)$$

where the summations range from j=1 to j=k. Thereby the estimated values of odds (W) and probabilities (P's) of participation in the commons are elicited.

The MCA table for adjusted values of P's is constructed by substituting appropriate combinations of ones, zeros, and mean values for the predictor variables (X_j's) in the above-mentioned estimated equations. The adjusted values are based on elicited parametric estimates for the complete model including all the predictors simultaneously. Alternatively, all the predictor variables are controlled at their mean values excepting the one whose effect is to be elicited at its particular level. The Multiple Classification Analysis (MCA) tables for the purpose are also presented in the study.

6.4 Why Individuals/Households Migrate

It was postulated that individual decisions to migrate depend on variables relating to

(a) asset ownership which is the primary determinant of expected income from private property as represented by ownership of agricultural land (HALO) and cattle (HSCU),
(b) remittances from towns (HRPM),

(c) infrastructural situation in the village, i.e., distance from nearest town (VDTC), connectivity by bus (VWCB) and existence of school (VASF), and

(d) levels and nature of institutional build-up in the village which determine the nature of rights in common property and therefore, the expected income from common property. This is represented by the dummy variables D1 and D2.

In other words, the nature of the source and the destination points for migration together determine the household decision regarding the division of the total labour available to them between work on assets within the village and for obtaining income from outside. Alternatively, a household may opt for daily commuting from the place of work in the city. In these areas, this provides a good alternative to distance migration, since it results in a kind of division of total family labour between the two areas. Therefore, both HMIG and HCOM are taken as the dependent variables. In the first set of results given in Table 6.1, intercept dummies defined as stated above, are intended to capture the impact of institution creation at the village level.

The parametric estimates relating to the variable HMIG, standing for distance migration are presented in Table 6.1. We find that the variable representing institutional build-up for a longer duration (D2)

TABLE 6.1
OLS Estimates of the Model with HMIG as the Response Variable

Variables	b's	t-Value
Institutional Build-up:		
Constant	21.227	1.723
D1	3.837	0.760
D2	−11.877	−1.506*
HLDW	0.008438	0.645
HLDL	−0.02715	−0.287
PVT. Assets Owned:		
HALO	−0.06200	−0.362
HSCU	−2.544	−2.690*
HRPM	0.0055	6.113*
Village Infrastructural:		
VWCB	1.737	0.324
VASF	−1.5082	−0.337
VDTC	−0.1727	−0.972
Statistics R^2= 42 N=182		

Note: *denotes significance at 1 per cent.

stalls distance migration significantly. The ownership of cattle (HSCU) also has a significant and negative effect on distance migration. As expected, the remittances sent home (HRPM) depict positive and significant impact on distance migration.

The other variables, such as distance from town (VDTC) and connectivity by bus (VWCB), though insignificant, depict expected directions of effects.

Daily commutation is also an important manner in which households try to supplement their income by dividing their labour force between working on assets in the village and wage labour elsewhere. The OLS specification with respect to this variable also gives results on lines similar to those of HMIG.

A perusal of Table 6.2 reveals that the impact of village level institution building on individual decision-making emerges after these institutions have worked in the villages for a period of around 10 years as shown by the negative and significant effect of D2 on HCOM. Again, households owning larger amounts of private agricultural land choose not to commute for wage labour. Connection by bus promotes commutation and larger distances from the town hinder the commutation process as expected.

TABLE 6.2
OLS Estimates of the Model with HCOM as the Response Variable

Variables	b's	t-Value
Institutional Build-up:		
Constant	150.77	3.358*
D1	100.44	5.480*
D2	−58.523	−2.035*
HLDW	−0.0455	−0.960
HLDL	−0.1627	−0.465
Ownership of Private Assets:		
HALO	−1.0303	−1.663*
HSCU	−0.4480	−0.130
HTCA	−0.0078	−0.044
Village Infrastructure Variables:		
VWCB	95.969	4.944
VASF	−59.8328	−3.682
VDTC	−2.1716	−3.344
Statistics $R^2 = .33$ N=186		

Note: *denotes significance at 1 per cent.

6.5 Why Households Participate in Commons (HPLI and HPWI)

The second behavioural decision of the household we consider is of whether or not to participate in the different activities that lead to creation of well-specified rights in common property. This decision strengthens the institutions created with outside intervention and is a measure of the extent to which institutional innovation has been internalised. Two possible kinds of participation are identified: that in the creation of common irrigation assets and that in the creation of rights in common land. In the case of irrigation structures, participation results in the creation of anicuts, tanks and other structures which lead to a sure supply of irrigation water, both directly and indirectly through a rise in the level of ground water in the region. The variable standing for effective participation in common irrigation structures or water resources (HPWI) states whether or not households decide to participate in this activity. The effective participation in common land resources (HPLI) on the other hand, states whether or not households participate in the creation of common property rights on land. This takes the form of ensuring rotational grazing and protecting land from encroachment by outsiders and others who do not have a right to it.

The estimated coefficients of the Logit Regression Model[5] for participation in commons, viz., common land resources (HPLI) and common water resources (HPWI), are presented in Tables 6.3 and 6.5, respectively. The estimated structural coefficients and their standard errors along with the levels of significance of different predictor variables for EPCLR are presented in Table 6.3.

A perusal of Table 6.3 reveals that all the estimated structural coefficients pertaining to institutional build-up of more than ten years in the villages (D2), participation in commons like common water resources (HPWI), ownership of cattle (HSCU) and extent of dependence on commons for cattle grazing (HCGC) have turned out to be highly significant. Furthermore, the direction of effects of all the predictor variables has turned out to be consistent with general expectations. Interestingly, longer and longer exposure of the villages to the institutional build-up initiated from outside by NGOs motivates people more and more to participate in the commons. Further, we find that participation in common land resources is found to be higher in villages which have been exposed to institutional build-up for longer

TABLE 6.3
Effect on Participation in Common Land Resources (HPLI):
Results of Logit Analysis

Predictor Variable	HPLI			
	Coefficients	Standard Errors	Level of Significance	Effect (Odd-Ratios)
D1	0.6704	0.7758	0.3875	1.9950
D2	1.0826	0.5790	0.0615*	2.9523
HPWI	0.9346	0.4724	0.0479*	2.5462
HPII	0.0000	0.0001	0.5101	1.0000
HALO	−0.0354	0.0322	0.2718	0.9652
HFMI	0.0001	0.0001	0.7634	1.0000
HSCU	0.3327	0.1951	0.0881*	1.3948
HCGU	0.0034	0.0018	0.0578*	1.0034
HFGC	0.0004	0.0016	0.8044	1.0004
SSHGO	−0.3845	0.3654	0.2927	0.6804
HMIG	−0.0104	0.0150	0.4848	0.9896
VWCR	0.2998	0.5782	0.6040	1.3497
Constant	−2.1051	0.8137	0.0097	
No of Observations	139			
−2 Log L1	165.08			
−2 Log L0	186.59			

Note: *denotes significance at 1 per cent.

durations (D2) compared to lesser durations (D1) or absolutely no exposure (the reference category depicted by the Constant). People participating in commons like common water resources also participate more in common land resources, could be because of complementarity reasons.

Ownership of cattle (HSCU) motivates persons to participate in the commons, i.e., common land resources like pasture lands, etc., basically because of the expectation of greater accessibility to fodder for their cattle stock. The positive linkage between the amount of cattle stock and participation in the common land resources also depicts more and more dependence on the commons for fodder, etc. This is reflected in the positive and significant association between the decision to participate in common land-based activity and extent of grazing of cattle owned in the common land areas (HCGC).

Interestingly, the directions of effects of all the other predictor variables, though not significant, have turned out to be consistent with the general expectations.

Estimated probabilities of participation in the common land resources are elicited through use of the estimated parameters and mean

TABLE 6.4
MCA Table of Adjusted Values of the Odds of Participation (W) and Probability of Participation (P) in Common Land Resources (HPLI)

Predictor Variable	Adjusted Value of	
	W	P
Institutional Development:		
Nil	0.415	0.293
Around 3–4 Yrs	0.812	0.448
Around 10+Yrs	1.226	0.550
Participation in Common Water Resources (HPWI):		
No	0.619	0.382
Yes	1.577	0.612
Cattle Ownership (HSCU):		
Nil	0.433	0.302
1	0.605	0.377
3	1.177	0.541
5	2.290	0.696
Cattle Grazing in Commons (HCGC):		
No	0.596	0.373
Average No of Days	0.753	0.429
Full Year	2.062	0.673

values of predictor variables and parametric estimates of the multivariate Logit models and the mean values of predictor variables presented in the appendix tables. The values are depicted as 'adjusted' since the values of the other predictors are kept at their mean values, excepting the predictor variable whose effect is to be highlighted. The adjusted values of the Odds (W's) and the probabilities (P's) of participation are presented in Table 6.4.

Perusal of the Table 6.4. reveals that extent of participation in the common land resources improves along with longer exposure of villages to institutional built-up. Interestingly, we find that participation rate in villages in commons like common land resources, which are not exposed to institutional built-up, is only around 29 per cent whereas it improves significantly to around 45 and 55 percentages in villages which are exposed for 3–4 years and more than 10 years, respectively.

Similarly, those who are participating in creation of common water resources (HPWI) like building of anicuts, nullah bunding, or dug wells, etc., are also participating more in management of common land resources. Rather, the probability of participation goes up from almost 38 per cent to 61 per cent amongst villagers who do not participate to those who participate in the management of common water resources.

Interestingly, we find that villagers with a higher ownership of cattle (HSCU) participate more in the management of common land resources. More specifically, the probability of participation improves from just around 30 per cent amongst villagers who do not own any cattle to almost 70 per cent among those who own five standard cattle units. Furthermore, those who depend more on common land resources for fodder for their cattle stock, obviously are supposed to be interested and participate more in the effective management and sustenance of common land resources and thus participate more in its management.

Turning now to participation in creation of common water resource management structures, the estimated structural coefficients and their standard errors along with the levels of significance of different predictor variables are presented in Table 6.5.

TABLE 6.5
Effect on Participation in Common Water Resources (HPWI):
Results of Logit Analysis

Predictor Variable	HPWI			
	Coefficients	Standard Errors	Level of Significance	Effect (Odd-Ratios)
D1	2.1587	1.2362	0.0808*	8.6596
D2	7.9562	19.2762	0.0798*	2853.1
HPII	0.0000	0.0001	0.4006	1.0000
HPAI	−0.1260	0.0711	0.0765*	0.8816
HALO	0.0181	0.0390	0.6424	1.01183
HTCA	−0.0056	0.0126	0.6552	0.9944
HSCU	0.0533	0.2124	0.8020	1.0547
HFMI	0.0000	0.0002	0.9491	1.0000
HMIG	−0.0035	0.0161	0.8293	0.9965
VASF	5.9502	19.2988	0.7578	383.84
VWCR	−6.5928	19.3083	0.7328	0.0014
Constant	−8.5376	19.2893	0.6580	

No of Observations 163
−2 Log L1 139.87
−2 Log L0 172.12

Note: *denotes significance at 1 per cent.

Table 6.5 reveals that exposure of villages to institutional build-up certainly helps in more and more participation in commons like common water resources, viz., anicuts, nullah bunding and dug wells. Both the dummies (D's) depicting the exposure of villages to the phenomenon of institutional built-up depict significant and positive impact on the participation of villages in the commons. Further, the magnitude of the coefficients also reveals that the longer duration of exposure helps better participation of villagers in the commons.

The availability of irrigational facilities through private resources or alternatively, private ownership of water resources, deters them from participating in the common water resources. The negative and significant association between privately-owned agricultural area already under irrigation (HPAI) and participation in common water resources (HPWI) clearly depict the phenomenon of lower participation by villagers who have or can manage more of their agricultural land holdings under irrigation.

Interestingly, the direction of effects of other predictor variables, which don't depict significant association, also turns out to consistent with the general expectations. More and more availability of migrational avenues (HMIG), connectivity of village by road which certainly improves the mobility of the villagers to avail employment opportunities in nearby or distant places reduces the possibility of participation in the commons.

Thus, most of the elicited parametric estimates depict the directions of effects to be consistent with the general expectations.

Estimated probabilities of participation in the common land resources are elicited through the use of estimated parameters in Table 6.6 and mean values of predictor variables and parametric estimates of the multivariate logit models and the mean values of predictor

TABLE 6.6
MCA Table of Adjusted Values of the Odds of Participation (W) and Probability of Participation (P) in Common Water Resources (HPWI)

Predictor Variable	*Adjusted Value of*	
	W	P
Institutional Development:		
Nil	0.002	0.002
Around 3–4 Yrs	0.018	0.017
Around 10+ Yrs	5.936	0.856
Privately-Owned Agricultural Land Under Irrigation (HPAI):		
Nil	0.099	0.090
5 Bighas	0.053	0.051
10 Bighas	0.028	0.027
20 Bighas	0.008	0.007

variables presented in the Appendix Tables. The values are 'adjusted' since the values of the other predictors are kept at their mean values excepting the predictor variable whose effect is to be highlighted. The adjusted values of odds (W's) and the probabilities (P's) of participation are presented in Table 6.6.

Perusal of Table 6.6 reveals that the participation rate improves significantly along with duration of exposure to the institutional build-up. Surprisingly, we find that the participation rate goes up almost from nil in villages with no institutional build-up to almost 86 per cent in villages which have been exposed to the build-up for more than 10 years. Thus, institutional build-up seems to be very important for motivating people to participate in commons.

As expected, we find that people who have private water resources or have more of their land under privately-owned irrigation resources are less likely to participate in the management of common water resources.

6.6 Magnitude of Participation in Commons

The decision of individuals on whether or not to participate is captured by the variables HPWI and HPLI. Further the degree of participation is measured by the number of labour days spent in the two kinds of participatory activity, that relating to creation of water-related assets (HLDW) and that relating to common land (HLDL). Another indirect measure could be the number of days of fodder collection through stall feeding (SFIP), one of the main modes of common land protection (as a substitute for grazing). The results with respect to magnitude of participation as measured by HLDW, HLDL and SFIP are discussed below and presented in Tables 6.7, 6.8 and 6.9, respectively.

The parametric estimates of extent of participation in common land resources (HLDL) are presented in Table 6.7. Interestingly we find that participation in land-related activity is explained significantly by the extent of dependence on common land as measured by the number of days of grazing in common land (HCGC).

It is also related positively to the participation in creation of common property in water (HLDW). Since the latter came earlier in point of time, this variable reflects the change in the village level institutional infrastructure as well.

TABLE 6.7
OLS Estimates of the Extent of Participation in
Common Land Resources (HLDL)

Predictor Variable	HLDL	
	Coefficient	t-Ratio
Constant	−11.533	−0.734
D1	−26.417	−1.40
D2	10.868	0.551
HLDW	0.44568	6.97
HSCU	0.02692	0.258
HFMI	0.004854	7.46
HMIG	0.08045	0.156
HCOM	0.0155	0.193
HCGC	0.080396	3.576

While cattle ownership (HSCU) does not turn out to be significant here, probably due to the inclusion of HCGC, the direction of the relationship is positive. Households having a higher level of income from sources other than agriculture, exhibit a larger extent of interest in participating in common water-related structures.

The estimated parameters for the extent of participation in common water resources (HLDW) are presented in Table 6.8.

TABLE 6.8
OLS Estimates of Extent of Participation in Common Water Resources (HLDW)

Predictor Variable	HLDW	
	Coefficient	t-Ratio
Constant	10.448	0.961
HLDL	0.49126	6.912
HALO	−0.26961	−0.262
HFMI	0.000128	0.140
HPII	0.000217	−0.262
FUEW	−2.9114	−0.570

When HLDW is taken as the measure of magnitude of participation, the only variable that emerges as significant is HLDL illustrating once again the complementarity between the two kinds of participation.

The extent of stall feeding (HSFI) as an indirect measure of participation with respect to land, gives some interesting results. This equation also has an explanatory power of about 57 per cent. Households with a higher level of income from non-agricultural sources (HFMI), also participate more. Participation is explained by the existence of a village-level institutional structure and by dependence on common land for cattle grazing. The estimated parameters for the structural relation with HSFI as response variable are presented in Table 6.9.

TABLE 6.9
OLS Estimates of Stall Feeding (HSFI)

Predictor Variable	SSFC	
	Coefficient	t-Ratio
Constant	0.63987	5.892
D1	−0.046702	−0.358
D2	0.19942	1.462
HLDW	0.003431	7.888
HSCU	−0.000044659	−0.062
HFMI	0.000042458	9.438
HMIG	0.0027992	0.787
HCOM	0.000066794	0.120
HCGC	0.0004014	9.438

6.7 Simultaneous Structural System

Thus far, decisions of households on whether to migrate, to commute to work daily from the village and/or to participate in strengthening village-level common property institutions have been analysed using a single equation approach, either as OLS or as a logit framework. This section sets up a simultaneous equations system to analyse decisions which are postulated to contain elements of inter-connectedness. The hypothesis is that in the presence of an innovative institution, each individual has to decide whether to migrate (either permanently or on a daily commutation basis) or to strengthen the institution by participating in the building-up of common property resources in the village economy. In the simultaneous system approach, it is postulated that the two decisions are taken in an interdependent fashion in the manner explained below.

The simultaneous structural system of formulated (hypothesised linkages between decision-making processes of migration and participation in commons) consists of three endogenous variables and nine exogenous variables. The three endogenous variables are distance migration (HMIG), number of labour days spent in protection of common land (HLDL) and in common water resources (HLDW). The nine exogenous variables are private ownership of agricultural land (HALO) and cattle stock (HSCU), private investments in irrigational sources (HPII), family's income from other non-agricultural sources (HFMI), remittances per month (HRPM), extent of dependence on common land for cattle grazing (HCGC), availability of schooling facility in the village (VASF), connectivity of village by bus (VWCB), and distance from the city (VDTC).

The specification of the structured system gets reflected in Table 6.10. The functional form of all the three structural relations is assumed to be intrinsically linear, i.e., linear in parameters. A perusal of

TABLE 6.10
3SLS Estimates of Structural Parameters of Migrational and Participation Response Variables in the Models in the Text

Var. Name	HMIG		HLDL		HLDW	
	Coeff.	t-value	Coeff.	t-value	Coeff.	t-value
Constant	10.50	1.19	−28.78	−1.67	−29.55	−0.65
D1	3.28	1.18	14.87	0.658	−36.63	−0.87
D2	−8.82	−1.551	23.87	1.111	18.98	0.384
HLDL	−0.0054	0.078				
HLDW	0.0015	−0.414	0.792	6.011		
HALO					−1.76	−0.436
D1HALO					10.14	2.37
D2HALO					1.69	0.395
PII					0.0012	2.97
D1PII					−0.0012	−2.16
D2PII					−0.00014	−0.054
HSCU					−6.28	−0.572
D1HSCU					4.22	0.276
D2HSCU					2.29	0.134
VASF					34.46	1.75
HFMI			0.0025	0.308	0.0029	0.301
D1HFMI			−0.0013	−0.160	−0.0017	−0.186
D2HFMI			0.0074	0.887	−0.0041	−0.416
HRPM	0.009	6.6225				
D1HRPM	−0.006	−3.594				
D2HRPM	0.007	1.047				
HCGC			0.114	4.16		
D1HCGC			−0.097	−2.43		
D2HGSC			−0.124	−2.003		
VWCB	0.111	0.647				
VDTC	−0.079	−0.439				

the system reveals that all the structural relations are over-identified and thus three stage least squares system estimational procedure (3SLS) is used for eliciting consistent estimates of the structural coefficients. Further, slope dummies for all independent variables are introduced together with intercept dummies to examine the effect of institution creation on migration and participation.

The estimated structural coefficients of the formulated simultaneous equations system by the system estimational procedure (3SLS) are presented in Table 6.10.

Perusal of the parametric estimates for HMIG in Table 6.10 reveals that the distress rural–urban migration process gets decelerated or stalled along with the process of institutional build-up in the rural areas as reflected by downward movement in the magnitude of the intercept dummies, i.e., from constant to D1 and D2. Also, we find that remittances to the households depict significant and positive impact on the extent of out-migration in villages with no institutional build-up, and it's significance and intensity of effect on out-migration gets reduced in villages with medium and longer duration of the institutional build-up. Thus, the process of distress migration from these villages gets stalled as institutions are built-up. Simultaneously, remittances lose their significance in the rural economy.

A perusal of the estimated coefficients of participation in common water resources (HLDW) in Table 6.10 reveals that it is higher in households having more of agricultural land (HALO) and irrigational sources (HPII) in these villages. It is possible that leadership for initiation of participation is provided by large asset-owners in the initial stages. However, we find that the ownership of private irrigational sources as reflected by private investments in irrigation (D1HPII) hinders participation in creation of common water resources in the medium and long run. Also we find that availability of schooling facility in the village (VASF) also depicts better participation in common water resources. Possibly, with some amount of literacy, the sensitisation of villagers to participation in creation of common water resources becomes easier.

The estimated coefficients of participation in common land resources (HLDL) reveal complementarity between participation in common water and common land resources. Alternatively, those who have participated more in creation of common water resources also depict a tendency to participate more in creation of common land resources.

Interestingly, it is observed that participation in creation of common land resources improves along with the duration of institutional build-up. Furthermore, households which depend more on common land for cattle grazing also participate more in creation of common land resources as revealed by significant and positive coefficient of extent of grazing by cattle (HCGC). The intensity of this linkage decreases over time as the institutional build-up takes place.

The estimated parameters of the formulated system of equations reveal strong inter-connections and multiple influences among the three crucial endogenous variables. Alternatively, the dynamic process of inter-connected decisions for migration and participation in commons gets reflected through those coefficients of the structured system which are significant.

6.8 Concluding Remarks

The analysis of migration, participation and institution creation within alternative frameworks of OLS, logit and simultaneous equations systems has yielded significant pointers to the direction of inter-relationships. It identifies variables one can expect to have positive and negative effects on individual and jointly-determined decisions with respect to the above. The study reveals that creation of common property rights in natural resource management stalls distance migration in the long run in a significant manner. The ownership of cattle stock also has significant and negative effect on distance migration. Furthermore, remittances sent home have positive and significant impact on distance migration. Also we find that households owning larger amounts of land don't choose to commute for wage labour. Connection by bus and all-weather road promotes commutation and large distances from nearby towns hinder it.

The availability of irrigation facilities through private resources or alternatively private ownership of water resources deters villagers from participating in common water resources. However, the institutional build-up in villages significantly improves participation of villagers in creation of common water resources like anicuts, nullah bunding and dug wells in the long run.

Ownership of cattle also motivates persons to participate in the commons, i.e., common land resources like pasture lands, etc., basically because of greater expectation of accessibility to fodder for their cattlestock. Also, the probability of participation in common land resources increases significantly amongst villagers who have participated in common water resources. It may be noted here that scarcity of water is so acute in arid and semi-arid zones of western India that accessibility to water is most important for the survival of humans as well as cattlestock. Water-related institutions can be expected to play the role of an entry point or catalyst in participatory processes.

The inter-connected nature of decision-making with respect to migration, commutation, and participation in commons, i.e., land and water resources, gets clearly reflected in the estimated structural coefficients of the formulated simultaneous structural system. The overall results reveal that,

(a) To begin with, participation in creation of common water resources is generally higher among the set of households owning more private land and cattlestock. However, the households with more of private sources of irrigation don't come forward for participation in creation of common water resources.

(b) The complementarity between participation in creation of common water and common land resources in the system also gets clearly revealed. Interestingly, participation in the commons improves significantly along with the exposure of the villages to the institutional build-up.

(c) The process of distress rural out-migration from the villages with no institutional build-up gets decelerated or stalled wherever creation of common property rights appears. Simultaneously, the significance of remittances gets reduced along with institutional build-up in the villages.

APPENDIX

TABLE A6.1
Household Level Variables

Migration Related:

HMIG	: Ratio of migrants to adult members above the age of fourteen.
HCOM	: Ratio of daily commuters to adult members of the family.
HREM	: Remuneration per household migrating into urban areas.
HRPM	: Remittance sent per month to household in village.

Asset and Income Related Variables:

HALO	: Private agricultural land owned.
HSCU	: Standard cattle units owned: The number of cattle owned are converted into standard units on the basis of ICAR norms.
HFMI	: Family income from sources other than agriculture.
HTCA	: Total cultivable land owned.
HPII	: Private investment in irrigation.
HPAI	: Privately-owned irrigated land.
HSFI	: Household stall feeding index.
HCGC	: No of days of common land grazing by cattle: an index of dependence on common land.
HFGC	: Forest grazing.
HCFC	: Collection fuelwood from forest and common land.

Institution Creation Variables:

HPWI	: Decision whether or not to participate in irrigation related institutions (has a 'yes-no' value).
HPLI	: Decision whether or not to participate in land-related institutions (has a 'yes-no' value).
HLDW	: Number of labour days spent (paid and unpaid) in working on water-related institutions.
HLDL	: Number of labour days spent (paid and unpaid) in working on land-related institutions.
SFIP	: Adoption of stall feeding as an indirect indicator of participation in institution creation.

Village Level Variables
Asset and Infrastructure-related Variables:

VLCL	: Village-level common land
VLFL	: Village-level forest land
VDTC	: Distance of village from city
VWCB	: Whether or not the village is connected by us
VWCR	: Whether or not the village is connected by road
VASF	: Availability of schooling facility in village

TABLE A6.2
Summary Statistics for the Selected Variables

No.	Variable	Unit	Mean	SD	Case
1.	HMIG	Per cent	7.2151	15.669	186
2.	HCOM	Per cent	52.009	58.776	186
3.	HREM	Rs per Month	1768.8	4237.5	205
4.	HRPM	Rs per Month	384.42	1167.7	205
5.	HALO	Bighas	5.6317	11.506	186
6.	HSCU	Standard Cattle Units	1.6559	1.1342	186
7.	HFMI	Rs per Annum	2740.1	12568	186
8.	HPII	Rs (once for all)	14408	29341	186
9.	HCGC	Number of Days per Annum	234.9	368.3	168
10.	HCFC	Yes/No. Answer	1.405	1.819	168
11.	HLDW	Number of Days per Year	20.435	128.19	186
12.	HLDL	Number of Days per Year	24.316	144.88	186
13.	SSFC	Number of Days Cattle Stall-fed			

TABLE A6.3
Summary Statistics for the Selected Variables of the G.K.Vas Village

No.	Variable	Unit	Mean	SD	Case
1.	HMIG	Per cent	0.67	3.65	30
2.	HCOM	Per cent	31.71	39.06	30
3.	HREM	Rs per Month	400.00	2190.89	30
4.	HRPM	Rs per Month	33.33	182.57	30
5.	HALO	Bighas	4.95	7.84	30
6.	HSCU	Standard Cattle Units	1.63	0.96	30
7.	HFMI	Rs per Annum	885.00	1018.55	30
8.	HPII	Rs (once for all)	4510.83	5760.32	30
9.	HCGC	Number of Days per Annum	17.50	45.27	30
10.	HCFC	Yes/No. Answer	0.97	0.18	30
11.	HLDW	Number of Days per Year	1.87	4.21	30
12.	HLDL	Number of Days per Year	1.77	3.92	30
13.	SFIP	Number of Days Cattle Stall-fed	0.83	0.38	30

TABLE A6.4
Summary Statistics for the Selected Variables of the Dhar Village

No.	Variable	Unit	Mean	SD	Case
1.	HMIG	Per cent	0.71	4.23	35
2.	HCOM	Per cent	76.12	48.10	34
3.	HREM	Rs per Month	0.00	0.00	35
4.	HRPM	Rs per Month	42.86	253.55	35
5.	HALO	Bighas	5.01	8.87	34
6.	HSCU	Standard Cattle Units	1.89	1.02	35
7.	HFMI	Rs per Annum	1078	1145.16	34
8.	HPII	Rs (once for all)	2701.47	2980.30	34
9.	HCGC	Number of Days per Annum	80.69	131.91	32
10.	HCFC	Yes/No. Answer	1.00	0.00	34
11.	HLDW	Number of Days per Year	2.00	6.28	35
12.	HLDL	Number of Days per Year	8.82	22.93	34
13.	SFIP	Number of Days Cattle Stall-fed	0.88	0.33	34

TABLE A6.5
Summary Statistics for the Selected Variables of the Majjam Village

No.	Variable	Unit	Mean	SD	Case
1.	HMIG	Per cent	5.93	14.45	30
2.	HCOM	Per cent	46.50	43.18	30
3.	HREM	Rs. per Month	1720.00	5464.52	30
4.	HRPM	Rs. per Month	203.33	504.11	30
5.	HALO	Bighas	4.17	3.51	30
6.	HSCU	Standard Cattle Units	1.80	1.21	30
7.	HFMI	Rs. per Annum	772.50	1001.60	30
8.	HPII	Rs. (once for all)	4980.00	4700.35	25
9.	HCGC	Number of Days per Annum	81.71	143.70	21
10.	HCFC	Yes/No. Answer	1.00	0.00	30
11.	HLDW	Number of Days per Year	0.00	0.00	30
12.	HLDL	Number of Days per Year	1.83	4.66	29
13.	SFIP	Number of Days Cattle Stall-fed	0.90	0.31	30

TABLE A6.6
Summary Statistics for the Selected Variables of the Bagdaunda Village

No.	Variable	Unit	Mean	SD	Case
1.	HMIG	Per cent	13.71	20.83	31
2.	HCOM	Per cent	31.18	52.15	31
3.	HREM	Rs per Month	1458.06	4230.43	31
4.	HRPM	Rs per Month	661.29	1568.37	31
5.	HALO	Bighas	2.87	2.47	31
6.	HSCU	Standard Cattle Units	1.26	1.09	31
7.	HFMI	Rs per Annum	1338.71	1757.78	31
8.	HPII	Rs (once for all)	4785.71	6244.15	28
9.	HCGC	Number of Days per Annum	98.08	123.65	30
10.	HCFC	Yes/No. Answer	0.89	0.31	28
11.	HLDW	Number of Days per Year	0.03	0.19	29
12.	HLDL	Number of Days per Year	2.23	4.77	30
13.	SSIP	Number of Days Cattle Stall-fed	0.77	0.43	30

TABLE A6.7
Summary Statistics for the Selected Variables of the Bunadia Village

No.	Variable	Unit	Mean	SD	Case
1.	HMIG	Per cent	10.53	16.27	30
2.	HRCOM	Per cent	32.29	34.92	30
3.	HREM	Rs per Month	2253.33	4087.98	30
4.	HRPM	Rs per Month	686.67	2189.12	30
5.	HALO	Bighas	6.47	5.91	30
6.	HSCU	Standard Cattle Units	1.70	1.29	30
7.	HFMI	Rs per Annum	1329.31	1578.29	29
8.	HPII	Rs (once for all)	7751.86	5778.62	22
9.	HCGC	Number of Days per Annum	67.00	131.85	26
10.	HCFC	Yes/No. Answer	1.00	0.00	30
11.	HLDW	Number of Days per Year	8.03	36.67	30
12.	HLDL	Number of Days per Year	0.53	1.83	30
13.	SFIP	Number of Days Cattle Stall-fed	0.83	0.38	30

TABLE A6.8
Summary Statistics for the Selected Variables of the Patia Village

No.	Variable	Unit	Mean	SD	Case
1.	HMIG	Per cent	12.60	20.64	30
2.	HCOM	Per cent	91.74	90.69	30
3.	HREM	Rs per Month	1960.00	3654.53	30
4.	HRPM	Rs per Month	186.67	320.27	30
5.	HALO	Bighas	4.17	3.67	29
6.	HSCU	Standard Cattle Units	1.67	1.21	30
7.	HFMI	Rs per Annum	1489.66	1889.32	29
8.	HPII	Rs (once for all)	4414.29	36.11	28
9.	HCGC	Number of Days per Annum	78.32	128.14	22
10.	HCFC	Yes/No. Answer	1.00	0.00	25
11.	HLDW	Number of Days per Year	15.03	51.45	29
12.	HLDL	Number of Days per Year	2.10	4.48	29
13.	SFIP	Number of Days Cattle Stall-fed	0.83	0.38	30

ENDNOTES

1. For details see, Saint, K. (1993).
2. It is to be noted that though an office existed within the bounds of Bagdaunda, people attending meetings and work done was more in Bunadia and Patia.
3. The number of cattle owned are converted to standard units using Indian Council of Agricultural Research (ICAR) norms.
4. For details, see Retherford and Minja (1993).
5. See the text for the main characteristics of the Logit Model.

Chapter 7
Summary and Policy Recommendations

7.1 Summary of Findings

This study addresses several critical inter connected issues relating to the creation of institutions for management of common property resources (CPRs), especially land and water, and people's decisions on rural–urban migration. The study highlights that people's decisions with respect to migration from a village are influenced, among other things, by whether or not well-specified rights to common property exist. This is because such a system of rights affects the magnitude and certainty with which income in cash or kind accrues from CPRs. This determines the total income and hence, the opportunity cost of migration.

The significance, magnitude and spatial distribution of CPRs, which have often been questioned by policy makers and programme implementors, are dealt with at the outset in the second chapter. It is found that the large magnitude of CPRs and its concentration in certain areas calls for a focused attention on institutions for their management. Alternate definitions of CPRs are examined in this same chapter. Correspondingly, magnitudes of regional CPRs are estimated using secondary data at the state level.

A clear distinction between wastelands and common property resources has also been made. While wasteland is an ecological category emerging out of a divergence between the actual and potential productivity of land, the nature of property rights in a resource determines whether it can be categorised as a CPR or not. This distinction between wasteland and common property resource is also dwelt upon in the second chapter. Utilising alternate data sets obtained from secondary and satellite sources, estimates of the two are also presented in the same chapter. It is interesting to note that these estimates are corroborated, by and large, by the first national level survey of CPRs conducted by the NSS organisation in 1998.

It is found that in certain ecosystems, for instance those in the arid and semi-arid parts of the country, the quantitative magnitude of common land resources (varying between 10 to 30 per cent of the geographical area in different states) is large implying that any change in their management will influence the welfare of people in rural areas of such states. This is particularly true at times of distress, especially in drought years, when common property resources assume special significance in providing consumption and income to distressed villagers. Such an importance is evidenced clearly in the emergence of a stream of distress migration from such regions wherever the degradation of CPRs renders them ineffective as an insurance cover for difficult times. The amply documented degradation of CPRs testifies that their role as a source of supplementary consumption and income during a drought is eroded and migration to urban areas is left as the only survival strategy for a large number of people. In this background, the present study highlights the effect of better management of CPRs in such situations. The study provides ample evidence that better management of CPRs can provide an alternate strategy for coping with such distress situations in the arid and semi-arid zones of India.

This study has as its starting point the well-documented evidence of extensive degradation of CPRs over the last two to three decades in different parts of India. Simultaneously, emergence of institutions for proper management of CPRs has been remarkable over the last decade or so, especially in areas where CPRs constitute a significant component of the overall resource base. Such institutions have tried to delineate property rights with respect to sets of resources in the specific local contexts in which they have been operating. The existence of such experiments enables the study to explore the links between better management of CPRs (interpreted as the creation of well-specified property rights in them) and changes in streams of distress migration to urban areas at different levels of aggregation in the chapters that follow.

The third chapter identifies three agro-climatic zones of the country corresponding to the arid and semi-arid zones as being significant from the viewpoint of the quantitative and qualitative importance of CPRs. A simultaneous equation system is set up with environmental degradation, stress migration from rural to urban areas and property rights changes in agricultural land over the eighties as endogenous variables. The model also identifies 11 exogenous socio-economic and developmental variables which are relevant for the system. The econometric database pertains to 89 districts spread over the three arid and semi-arid agro-climatic zones in the western part of India. The parametric estimates are elicited through system method of estimation and are discussed in the same chapter. The estimates highlight that distress migration is influenced by factors impinging on the profitability of agriculture and by the magnitude of common land resources. Higher irrigational intensity, higher land productivity and regeneration of forests reduce stress migration from the rural tracts. Shrinkage of common land area and a deteriorating physical environment result in a larger outflow of people to urban areas. These results are more or less in conformity with the findings of several other micro-level studies.

The fourth chapter investigates the changes that take place in particular locales where a better management of CPRs is attempted. This chapter also dwells at length on the question of how NGO initiatives emerge. The district of Udaipur, located within the arid and semi-arid zone of western India and home to 15 major initiatives in the area of land and water management, is selected for this study. Two kinds of evolutionary patterns are discerned—both dependent for initiation on urban support. In one pattern, the evolution is from a broad base of interest in problems of rural development to environmental upgradation, typically with reference to land and water management issues. In the second situation, a focused interest on a sector of special importance in the countryside is the starting point.

A common feature of both kinds of evolution is the dependence on sources of funding outside of the communities in which the intervention is planned. While this is an essential ingredient in the early phases of work in a less developed region, the question invariably arises: at what phase, and how, will local value addition generate sufficient surplus for such organisations to be self-sufficient?

Five projects where changes in management of CPRs have been attempted are selected for the study. The analysis reveals a significant association between different qualitative attributes of the micro-level projects under study in the chapter. It finds that decrease in out-migration is significantly associated with creation of property rights, environmental upgradation and participatory development. However, differences in levels of resource endowment as between different entities do not seem to affect this phenomenon. The change has taken place in villages with low levels of resource endowment as well as in those with higher levels.

The next part of the study covering the fifth and sixth chapters is an evaluation of the impact of a particular NGO initiative in the specific context of the questions asked and the hypothesis framed at the outset. Six villages in the tehsils of Gogunda and Girwa at distances varying from 20 to 70 kilometres from Udaipur are selected for this analysis. In order to capture the impact of the institutional innovation initiated by the NGO, the villages are divided into three broad categories:

1. those in which NGOs have been working for over a decade,
2. those where the institutions have been in existence only for about three to five years, and
3. those where there has been very little or almost no intervention.

The fifth chapter provides an overview of the six tribal villages selected for in-depth study in Udaipur district and surrounding Udaipur city. Though the villages are very similar in terms of the resource base measured by the land and livestock ownership, they do differ with respect to magnitude of out-migration as well as daily commutation and also with respect to the indices for environmental variables such as depth of ground water table and forest degradation.

The sixth chapter constitutes an econometric exploration into the processes of institutional intervention, people's participation in creation and protection of common land and water resources, and their decisions on migration. The process of institution creation in the six villages in terms of protection of common pasture and building of common irrigation sources are discussed at length in the chapter.

In the simultaneous equation system, it is hypothesised that the decision to migrate and the decision to participate in commons-related activities in the village are taken simultaneously by the household.

These are in fact two aspects of the decision with respect to allocation of labour between village-focused activities and work outside of the village economy.

The econometric analysis and empirical evidence in the study reveal that creation of common property rights significantly stalls distance migration in the long run. The ownership of cattlestock also has a significant and negative effect on distance migration. Furthermore, remittances sent home have a positive and significant impact on distance migration. Also we find that households owning larger amounts of land don't choose to commute for wage labour. Connection of the village by bus and all-weather road promotes commutation and large distances from nearby towns hinder commutation process.

The availability of irrigational facilities through private resources or alternatively, private ownership of water resources, deters villagers from participating in institutions for the creation of common water resources. However, the institutional build-up in villages significantly improves participation of villagers in creation of common water resources for people not having access to their own irrigation sources.

Ownership of cattle also motivates persons to participate in the commons, i.e., in common land resources like pasture lands. This is basically because of the expectation of greater accessibility to fodder for their cattlestock. Also, the probability of participation in common land resources increases significantly amongst villagers who have participated in common water resources. It may be noted here the scarcity of water is so acute in arid and semi-arid zones over western India that accessibility to water is most important for the survival of humans as well as cattlestock. It often acts as the entry point or the catalyst for initiating the process of change.

The dynamic process of decision-making with regard to migration, commutation and participation in commons, i.e., land and water resources, gets clearly reflected in the estimated structural coefficients of the formulated simultaneous structural system. The results reveal that to begin with, the participation in creation of common water resources is generally higher from households with more private ownership of land and cattlestock. However, households with more private sources of irrigation do not come forward for participation in creation of common water resources. The complementarity between participation in creation of common water and common land resources in the system is also clearly revealed. Interestingly, participation in the commons improves significantly along with the exposure of the villages to the institutional build-up. The process of distress rural outmigration from villages with no institutional build-up gets decelerated or stalled when creation of common property rights takes place. Simultaneously, the significance of remittances is reduced along with institutional build-up.

To reiterate, the findings of the study indicate that:

1. Rural–urban migration gets decelerated with increased institutional intervention, as indicated by downward movement in the direction of the institutional dummy variables.
2. Participation in common water resources seems to be higher by households having larger land and livestock but a low level of private investment in irrigation. This indicates that leadership in participation comes from the large asset-owner if a complementarity exists between his resource base and the inputs provided by the new institution.
3. Further, participation in common land is complementary with that in water. This seems to indicate a kind of snowballing effect, after a certain level of awareness has been created.

7.2 Policy Implications

Non-governmental initiatives in development have grown in India in the last two decades. This growth had its origin in the interest of city-based persons and organisations in the problems of the countryside and was supported by government, non-government and international aid granting institutions. In a large number of cases, problems relating to land and water management emerged as the focal point of intervention, particularly in arid and semi-arid regions. This study attempts to document the impact of such intervention in the larger context of the issues of environmental degradation and migration from rural areas.

Policy implications emerging from this study can be viewed at two levels. The first set of recommendations is related to the specific issue of migration and the creation of property rights. As outlined above, the issue has been examined from a number of alternative viewpoints. Indications are that distress migration in arid and semi-arid tracts can be contained by improving the management of common property resources. Once a proper system of right to use and obligation to protect is in place, income and consumption from these resources accrues with a greater degree of certainty. They can be depended upon to provide sustenance in times of need. The opportunity cost of migration rises and its significance as a survival strategy decreases.

Further, a household-level study in six villages with different levels of institutional intervention examines the different aspects of the house decision to allocate labour between village and non-village based economic activity. Here, interesting linkages between ownership of private resources and participation in institutions for managing common pool resources arise. Large landowners who tend to gain from activities that augment water resources participate in institutions improving their management. However, they do so only when they do not have private sources of irrigation. This seems to be logical and points towards the kind of group that institutions for land and water management can look to for providing leadership.

The findings of this study can also be viewed in the broader perspective of the course that development is taking in India at the turn of the century. While one section of the economy in moving towards globalisation based on a liberalisation programme, the need for providing safety nets for about one-third of the population which is likely to be left out of such a movement has been underscored from the start of the changed programme. One form that such safety nets take is that of creation of viable institutions that serve to allocate and manage resources in sectors where the market does not perform this role effectively and efficiently. The experience of local institutions for natural resource management and the lessons to be learnt from it are crucial in this context.

Interestingly, most institutions for the management of rural resources originate in an urban context. This is understandable, given the relatively low level of human and financial resources available in rural areas. The issue of ensuring that such institutions become self-reliant is important. This can happen if a part of their activities are of the kind that have market linkages and are value-adding at the local level. Such an orientation has not been given much significance as of now but needs to be attended to.

Another important aspect is that of the focus with which alternative institutional structures are initiated. The present study corroborates that the focus needs to be one of perception of local issues at a decentralised level. Starting with a general centralised view of rural development only tends to extend the exploratory phase of institution creation.

It is important to understand, in the wider framework of development at the national level, that development processes must be dispersed. Rural development and environmental upgradation are not only desirable objectives for their own sake but would also prevent the continuous degradation in the state of the urban environment in which a continuous stream of migration tends to create shanty towns without basis amenities on the outskirts of large cities.

References

Agarwal, Anil and Narain, Sunita (1971), 'A Regression Analysis of Migration to Urban Areas of a Less Developed Country: The Case of India', *Journal of Regional Science*, 11(2), pp. 253–62.
—— (1989), *Towards Green Villages, A Strategy for Environmentally Sound and Participatory Rural Development*. New Delhi: Centre for Science and Environment.
—— (1992), 'Environment and Development: Traditions, Concerns and Efforts in India', Report submitted to the United Nations Conference on Environment and Development, p. 41. Ahmedabad: Centre for Environment Education.
Bagchi, K. S. and Philips, M. (1993), *Wastelands in India: An Untapped Potential*. Upalabdhi. New Delhi: Trust for Developmental Initiatives.
Bahuguna, V. K. (1992), *Collective Resource Management; An Experience in Harda Forest Division*. Bhopal: Regional Centre For Wasteland Development (RCWD), Indian Institute of Forest Management.
Benneh, G. (1994), 'Environmental Consequences of Different Patterns of Urbanisation', in *Population, Environment and Development*, p. 159. New York: United Nations, Department of Economic and Social Information and Policy Analysis.
Berkes, F. (ed.) (1989), *Common Property Resources—Ecology and Community Based Sustainable Development*. London: Belhaven Press.
Bhumbla, D. R. and Khare A. (undated), 'Estimates of Wastelands in India'. New Delhi: Society for Promotion of Wasteland Development.
Bowonder, B., Prasad, S. S. R. and Unni, N. V. M. (1987), 'Afforestation in India', *Land Use Policy*, 4(2), pp. 133–46.
Bromley, Daniel (1989), *Economic Interests and Institutions, The Conceptual Foundations of Public Policy*. Oxford and New York: Basil Blackwell.
—— (1991), *Environment and Economy: Property Rights and Public Policy*. Cambridge, Mass.: Basil Blackwell.
—— (1992), 'The Commons, Common Property and Environmental Policy', *Environmental and Resource Economics*, 2(1), pp. 1–17.
Burra, Neera (1991), *Women and Wasteland Development: A Review of N.G.O. Experience*, Programme On Rural Employment And Development Department. Geneva: International Labour Organisation.
Census of India (1971, 1981 & 1991), *Provisional Population Totals: Rural-Urban Distribution*. India: Registrar General and Census Commissioner.
—— (1989), *Child Mortality, Age at Marriage and Fertility in India*, Occasional paper No. 2 (1989). India: Registrar General and Census Commissioner.

Census of India (1991), *Provisional Population Totals: Workers and Their Distributions*. Paper 3 of 1991, India: Registrar General and Commissioner.

—— (1991), *Provisional Population Totals: Rural-Urban Distribution*, Paper 2 of 1991, India: Registrar General and Census Commissioner.

Centre for Monitoring Indian Economy (CMIE) (1982), *District Level Data for Key Economic Indicators*. Bombay: The Center for Monitoring Indian Economy.

—— (1987), *District Level Data for Key Economic Indicators*. Bombay: The Center for Monitoring Indian Economy.

Centre for Science and Environment (1982), *The State of India's Environment*, Volume II. New Delhi.

Chopra, Kanchan (1993a), 'Sustainability of Agriculture', *Indian Journal of Agricultural Economics*, July-Sept, 48 (3), pp. 527-35.

—— (1993b), 'Sustainable Development: Some Interpretations and Applications in the Context of Indian Agriculture', *Structural Change and Economic Dynamics*, 4(1), pp. 183-97.

—— (1996), 'The Management of Degraded Land: Issues and an Analysis of Technological and Institutional Solutions', *Indian Journal of Agricultural Economics*, Jan-June, 51(1&2), pp. 238-48.

—— (1998), 'Watershed Management Programmes: An Evaluation of Alternative Institutional and Technological Options'. Working paper No: E/197/98/. Delhi: Institute of Economic Growth.

Chopra, Kanchan, and Rao, C. H. H. (1992), 'The Links Between Sustainable Agricultural Growth and Poverty', *Quarterly Journal of International Agriculture*, Oct-Nov, 31(4), pp. 365-77.

—— (1997), 'Institutional and Technological Perspectives on the links between Agricultural Sustainability and Poverty: Illustrations from India,' in Stephen Vosti and Thomas Reardon (ed.), *Sustainability, Growth and Poverty Alleviation*. Boltimore, Maryland: IFPRI and Johns Hopkins Press.

Chopra, Kanchan and Gulati, S.C. (1993), 'Population, Poverty and Environmental Degradation: The Role of Property Rights', Background Paper, World Resource Institute, Second India Revisited Study. Delhi: Institute of Economic Growth.

—— (1997a), 'Environmental Degradation and Population Movements: The Role of Property Rights,' *Environment and Resource Economics* 9(1), pp. 383-408.

—— (1997b) 'Population, Poverty and Environmental Degradation: The Role of Property' in Anil Agarwal (ed.), *'The Challenge of the Balance: Environmental Economics in India: Proceedings of a National Environment and Economics Meeting'*. New Delhi: Centre for Science and Environment.

—— (1998), 'Environmental Degradation, Property Rights and Population Movements: Hypotheses and Evidences from Rajasthan,' *Environment and Development Economics* 31, pp. 35-57.

Chopra, Kanchan, and Kadekodi, G. K. (1993), 'Watershed Development: A Contrast with NREP/JRY', *Economic and Political Weekly*, June 26, 28(26), pp. A-61-A-67.

—— (1999), *Operationalising Sustainable Development: Economic Ecological Modelling for Developing Countries*. Indo-Dutch Studies on Development Alternatives, 22. New Delhi: Sage Publications.

Chopra, Kanchan, Kadekodi, G. K. and Murty, M. N. (1990), *Participatory Development: People and Common Property Resources*. New Delhi: Sage Publications.

Cincotti, R. and Pangare, G. (1993), 'Pastoralists: Brokers of Agricultural Soil Fertility', *Wasteland News*, 8(3), p. 40.

References

Ciriacy-Wanthrop, S. V. and Bishop, R. C. (1975) 'Common Property as a Concept in Natural Resource Policy,' *Natural Resources Journal*, 15(4), pp. 713–27.

Cohen, J. E. (1995), *How Many People Can the Earth Support*. New York: W. W. Norton and Company.

Collins, N. Mark, Sayer, Jeffrey A. and Whitmore, Timothy C. (1991), *The Conservation Atlas of Tropical Forests: Asia and the Pacific*. London and Basingstoke: Macmillan Press.

Commander, Simon (1986), 'Managing Indian Forests: A Case for the Reform of Property Rights', *Development Policy Review*, 4, pp. 328–29.

Connell, J., Dasgupta, B., Laishley, R. and Lipton, M. (1975), *Migration from Rural Areas: The Evidence from Village Studies*. University of Sussex: Institute of Development Studies, Discussion Paper No. 39.

Cruz, M. C., Meyer, C. A., Reppeto, R. and Woodward, R. (1992), *Population Growth, Poverty and Environmental Stress: Frontier Migration in the Philippines and Costa Rica*. Washington D.C: World Resources Institute.

Development Alternatives (1988), *Common Property Resources Management*, Study in Ajmer and Jodhpur districts, Rajasthan. New Delhi: Development Alternatives.

Gadgil, M. (1992), '*State Subsidies and Resource Use in a Dual Society*,' in Anil Agarwal (ed.) 'The Price of Forests'. New Delhi: Centre For Science and Environment.

Gera, Prema (undated), *Farmers' Participation in Externally Catalysed Irrigation System. The Case of The Johads*. (Mimeo). New Delhi: Development Alternatives.

Government of India (1968–69), *Forest Statistics of India*. New Delhi: Directorate of Economic and Statistics, Ministry of Agriculture.

—— (1970–71 & 1980–81), *Agriculture Census*. New Delhi: Agricultural Census Division, Ministry of Agriculture.

—— (1975), *The Gazetteer of India, Economic Structure and Activity, II*. New Delhi: Ministry of Education and Social Welfare.

—— (1984), *Report of the Committee for Review of Rights and Commissions in the Forest Area of India*. New Delhi: Department of Agriculture and Cooperation, Ministry of Agriculture.

—— (1989a), *Fertility in India*, Occasional Paper No. 2 of 1989, Demographic Division. India: Registrar General and Census Commissioner.

—— (1989b), *Developing India's Wastelands*. New Delhi: Ministry of Environment and Forests.

—— (1991), *The State of Forest Report*. Dehra Dun: Ministry of Environment and Forests.

—— (1992a), *National Watershed Development Project for Rainfed Areas*. New Delhi: Department of Agriculture and Cooperation, Ministry of Agriculture.

—— (1992b), *Soil Conservation in the Catchments of River Valley Projects*. New Delhi: Department of Agriculture and Cooperation, Ministry of Agriculture.

—— (1995), *Report on Area Statistics of Land-use/Land Cover Generated Using Remote Sensing Techniques*. Hyderabad: Department of Space, National Remote Sensing Agency.

—— (Different Years), *Agricultural Statistics of India*. New Delhi: Directorate of Economics and Statistics, Ministry of Agriculture.

Greenwood, M. (1971a), 'An Analysis of the Determinants of Internal Labour Mobility in India', *Annals of Regional Science*, 5(1), pp. 137–51.

—— (1971b), 'A Regression Analysis of Migration to Urban Areas of a Less Developed Country: The Case of India', *Journal of Regional Science*, 11(2), pp. 253–62.

Gulati, S. C. (1992), 'Developmental Determinants of Demographic Variables in India: A District Level Analysis', *Journal of Quantitative Economics*. 8(1), pp. 157–72.

Gulati, S. C. (1993), *Population Growth Potential: A District Level Analysis.* (Mimeo). New Delhi: Institute of Economic Growth.

Gulati, S. C. and Chopra, Kanchan (1994), 'Population Redistribution, Environmental Degradation and Landuse Patterns: A District Level Study of Linkages in Arid and Semi-arid Zones of India', *Demography India,* 23(1&2), pp. 1–14.

Haagenson, Jan Ole (1998), 'The Adaptive State? Joint Forest Management in Madhya Pradesh', Paper presented at Workshop on Shared Resource Management in South Asia. Anand, the Institute of Rural Management.

Harman, Harry (1960), *Modern Factor Analysis.* Chicago: Chicago University Press.

Intriligator, Michael D. (1980), *Econometric Models, Techniques, and Applications.* New Delhi: Princeton Hall of India Pvt. Ltd.

Jodha, N. S. (1983), *Market Forces and Erosion of Common Property Resources.* ICRISAT, P. O. Patancheru, Hyderabad: Proceedings of International Workshop, October.

—— (1985), 'Population Growth and the Decline of Common Property Resources in Rajasthan, India', *Population and Development Review,* 11(2), pp. 247–64.

—— (1986), 'Common Property Resources and the Rural Poor in Dry Regions of India', *Economic and Political Weekly,* July 5, 30(27), pp. 1169–81.

—— (1991), *Environmental Concerns and Common Property Resources: Missing Dimensions.* (Mimeo). Kathmandu: International Centre for Integrated Mountain Development.

Jones, G. (1993), 'Remembrances of Times Past: The Experiences of Sewa Mandir's and Vidya Bahwan's Early Volunteers', *Sewa Mandir Newsletter,* Jan-March, pp. 24–27.

Kadekodi, G. K. (1994), *Resource and Livelihood Linkages: The Context of Operationalising Sustainable Development.* (Mimeo). New Delhi: Institute of Economic Growth.

—— (1997), *Valuation of CPR Management: Regeneration with Community Involvement.* (Mimeo). New Delhi: Institute of Economic Growth.

Kadekodi, G. K. and Chopra, Kanchan (1990), 'Cyclical Re-investment Strategy: An Alternative Approach To Rural Development', *Social Action,* 40(4), pp. 382–98.

Kadekodi, G. K. and Perwaiz, Aslam (1998), *Dimensions of Wasteland and Common Property Resources in India.* New Delhi: Institute of Economic Growth Working Paper No. E/190/98.

Kirk, R. Smith (1987), *Biofuels, Air Pollution, and Health: A Global Review.* New York: Plenum Press.

Kolavalli, Shashi (1997), 'Assessing Water Users Associations', Paper presented at Workshop on Agriculture and the Environment. Delhi: Delhi School of Economics.

Kumar, Arun (1992), Technological options for lands in Rajasthan. (Mimeo report). New Delhi: Society for Promotion of Wasteland Development.

Larson, B. A. and Bromley, D. W. (1990), 'Property Rights, Externalities and Resource Degradation, Locating the Tragedy', *Journal of Development Economics* 33(2), pp. 235–62.

Lipton, M. (1976), 'Migration from Rural Areas of Poor Countries: The Impact on Rural Productivity and Income Distribution'. Paper presented at Research Workshop on Rural Labour Market Interactions. Washington D. C.: International Bank for Reconstruction and Development.

Madhav Tailor and Rathore, M. S. (1993), 'The Story of Barava', *Sewa Mandir News Letter,* April-June 1993, pp. 19–20.

Maheshwari, R. C., Singh, D. P. and Ambekar, V. M. (1990), *A Case Study of Irrigated Watershed Management. Tejpura, Jhansi,* Kanpur: Third IWRS National Symposium on Water shed Development and Management.

Malik, R. P. S. and Faeth Paul (1993), 'Rice-Wheat Production in Northwest India', in Paul Faeth (ed.), *Agricultural Policy and Sustainability: Case Studies from India, Chile, the Philippines and the United States*, pp. 17–31. Washington, D. C.: World Resources Institute.

Mencher, Joan (1999), 'NGOs: Are They a Force For Change?', *Economic and Political Weekly*, July 24, 1999, pp. 2081–86.

Ministry of Environment and Forests (MOE), India (1991), The State of Forest Report, 1991, pp. 7. Dehra Dun: Ministry of Environment and Forests.

Ministry of Health and Family Welfare (1987), *District-Wise Couple Protection Rates: As on 31st March 1987*. New Delhi: Evaluation and Intelligence Division. Ministry of Health and Family Welfare.

Mohan, Rakesh (1992), 'Population and Urbanisation: Strategies to Cope with City Growth', in Vasant Gowariker (ed.), *Science, Population and Development*, pp. 244–72. Pune: Unmesh Communications.

National Centre For Human Settlements and Environment (1987), *Documentation on Forests and Rights, Volumes 1 and 2*. New Delhi.

National Sample Survey (1999), *Common Property Resources*, NSS 54th Round, (Jan-June 1998), Draft Report No. 452(54/3.3/31). NSS Organisation. New Delhi: Department of Statistics, Government of India.

Ostrom, E. (1990), 'Governing The Commons: The Evolution of Institutions for Collective Action' in James E Alt and Douglas C North (ed.), *Political Economy of Institutions and Decisions*. U.S.A.: Cambridge University Press.

Pangare, Ganesh and Pangare, V. (1992), *From Poverty To Plenty, The Story of Ralegaon Siddhi*. New Delhi: Indian National Trust For Art and Cultural Heritage.

Parikh, J., Parikh, K., Gokharan, S., Painuly, J. P., Saha, B., and Sukhla, V. (1991), *Consumption Patterns: The Driving Force For Environmental Stress*. Bombay: Indira Gandhi Institute of Development Research.

Planning Commission, Agroclimatic Regional Planning Unit (1993), *Agroclimatic Regional Planning District Level*, Working Paper No. 7, ARPU. New Delhi.

Premi, M. K. (1991), *India's Population: Heading Towards a Billion*. Delhi: B. R. Publishing Corporation.

Quiggin, John (1993), 'Common Property, Equality and Development', *World Development Report*, 21(7), pp. 1123–38.

Rao, C. H. H. (1990), 'Some Inter-relationships between Agricultural Technology, Livestock Economy, Rural Poverty and Environment: An Inter-State Analysis for India', *Golden Jubilee Volume of Indian Society of Agricultural Economics*.

Repetto (1994), 'The Second India Revisited: Population, Poverty, and Environmental Stress over Two Decades', p. 37, p. 82. Washington D.C.: World Resources Institute.

Repetto, R. and Gills, M. et al (1988), *Public Policies and the Misuse of Forest Resources*, Washington D.C.: World Resources Institute.

Repetto, R., and Holmes, T. (1983), 'The Role of Population in Resource Depletion in Developing Countries', *Population and Development Review*. 9 (4); pp. 609–32.

Retherford, Robert D. and Minja, Kim Choe (1993), *Statistical Models for Casual Analysis*. New York: John Wiley & Sons Inc.

Saint, Kishore (1993), *Social Dynamics of Natural Resources Management–A Case Study in South Rajasthan Aravallis*. Udaipur: Ubeshwar Vikar Mandal.

Seldon, T. M. and D. S. Song (1994), 'Environmental Quality and Development: Is There a Kuznets Curve for Air Pollution Emissions?', *Journal of Environmental Economics and Management* 27(2), pp. 147–62.

Sethi, G. (1994). 'Degradation of the Soil Resource' New Delhi: Tata Energy Research Institute Draft Paper, p. 3.

Sewa Mandir Annual Report 1991–92. Udaipur: Sewa Mandir.

Shafik, N. and Bandhopadhyay, S. (1992), 'Economic Growth and Environmental Quality: Time Series and Cross-Country Evidence'. Washington: World Bank Working Papers, WPS 904.

Shah, Tushar, Sreenivasan, R., Shanmugam, C. R. and Vasimalai, M. P. (1998), 'Sustaining Tamilnadu's Tanks' in D. K. Marothia (ed.), *Institutionalising Common Pool Resources.* New Delhi: Concept Publishing Company.

Society for Promotion of Wasteland Development (1989), *A Study of Jawaja Project.* New Delhi.

Srinivasan, K. (1993), *Demographic Transition in India Since 1970: Trends and Correlates,* Background Paper. Washington D.C.: World Resources Institute, Second India Revisited Study.

Tata Services (1992), 'Statistical Outline of India'. Bombay.

The Imperial Gazetteer of India (1907), *The Indian Empire Economic,* III. Oxford: The Clarendon Press.

Todaro, M. P. (1980), 'Internal Migration in Developing Countries: A Survey', in A. Easterlin (ed.), Population and Economic Change in Developing Countries. Chicago: University of Chicago Press.

United Nations and World Health Organisation Environment Programme (1992), *Urban Air Pollution in Megacities of the World.* Oxford: Blackwell.

United Nations (1994), *Population, Environment and Development: Proceedings of the United Nations Expert Group Meeting.* New York: Department of Economic and Social Information and Policy Analysis.

Wade, Robert (1988), *Village Republics: Economic Conditions for Collective Action in South India.* Cambridge: Cambridge University Press.

White, T. A. and Runge, C. F. (1994), 'Common Property and Collective Action: Lessons from Cooperative Watershed Management in Haiti', Chicago: *Economic Development and Cultural Change,* 43(1), pp. 1–41.

—— (1995), 'The Emergence and Evolution of Collective Action: Lessons from Watershed Management in Haiti', *World Development,* 23 (10), pp. 1683–98.

World Bank (1992), *World Development Report, Development and the Environment.* New York: Oxford University Press.

World Wide Fund for Nature (India) (1994), *Environmental N.G.O's in India: A Directory.* New Delhi.

World Resources Institute (WRI) (1995), *World Resources: A Guide to the Global Environment.* pp. 83–106. Delhi: Oxford University Press.

Index

agricultural land, 37, 39
agro-climatic zones, characteristics of, 47
arid and semi-arid regions: study of property rights at district level in, 44–72; characteristics of, 47, demographic variables, 40–49; employment related variables, 50, factor analysis of interlinkages, 51–52; 60–70; factor structure for 52–54; impact multipliers, 63–65; livestock related variables 50, natural resource variables, 49–50; parametric estimates of the model, 61–63; region of study, 45–48; simultaneous structural system for, 54–57; structural relations, 57–61; 70–72; summary and conclusions of study 65–66; variables for, 48–51; 67

Bagdaunda village study, *see*, villages of Udaipur district studied
barren and unculturable land, 37
barren rocky land, 41
Bunadia village study, *see*, Villages of Udaipur district studied

CAPART, 81
canal, 41
carrying capacity concept, 19–20
common land resources: effect on participation in, 130; extent of participation, 135; probability of participation, 131
common property resources (CPRs): alternative estimates, 33–35; component of, 27–28; definition, 28–29; degraded land and, 33; identification of, 26; in India, 22–36; land and wasteland, 31–33; land use classification, 24–25; methodology for estimating 26–33; policy formulation for, 35–36; property right arrangement, 22–23; statewise magnitude of, 29–30; wasteland and land under, 31–33
common water resources : effect on participation, 132; extent of participation, 135; probability for participation, 133
crop land, 39
culturable wasteland, 38
current fallow land, 38

DRDA, 86
deciduous forest, 39
degraded forest, 39
Dhar village study, *see*, Villages of Udaipur district studied

environmental degradation, in Villages of Udaipur, 44–72
evergreen forest, 39

fallow land, 38–39

forests, 39
forest blank, 40
forest land, 37
forest plantations, 40

Gahaloton Ka Vas (G.K.Vas) village, *see,* Villages of Udaipur district studied
Gati Bimal, 80
glacial area, 41
grassland, 41
grazing land, 37,41
greenwood, 18
gullied land, 40

Harman, Harry, 51
industrial wasteland, 42
intriligator, 61

Kuznets, 13–14

lakes, 41
land put to agricultural uses, 37,39
land under miscellaneous tree-crops, 37
land use classification: based on land utilisation purposes, 37–38; classes definition, 37–38;of CPR, 24–25; using remote sensing technique, 39–42
land with/without scrub, 40–41

Majjam village study, *see,* Villages of Udaipur district studied
Magrove, 40
marshy land, 40
Mehta, Mohan Sinha, 81
migration pattern; in villages of Udaipur, 18–20, 44–72, 117–72
mining wasteland, 42
Mohan Singh Mehta Centre for Training, Kaya, 81
National Remote Sensing Agency (NRSA) 25, 28, 31

National resource management institutions: tasks before to address, 14–15
National Wasteland Development Board (NWDB), 25, 31–32, 82
Net Area Sown (NAS) land, 38

Patia village study, *see,* Villages of Udaipur district studied
permanent pastures and other grazing land, 37
plantations, 39
poverty: environment degradation and, 13–17
property rights: arrangements, 22–23; environmental degradation and, 44–72; factor analysis for, 51–52, 68–70; rural–urban migration, and, 18–20,44–72; structures, 16–18, 57–61, 70–72; study of in arid and semi–arid region, 44–72

Rajasthan, indices for, 98
ravinous land, 40
reservoir, 41
river, 41

SWACH, 81
Saaksharta Sandesh, 80
salt–affected land, 40
salt pans, 42
sandy area, 41
Save Aravalli Campaign, 85
Scrub, 39
semi–arid zones: micro–level initiatives in, 73–101; alternative interventions, 87–94; characteristics of selected projects, 89–94; evolution of, 74–75; impact assessment, 94–97; NGO intervention in, 77–87, 98–101; organisations and institutions, 75–87,—.

Sewa Mandir, 78–84; Ubeshwar Vikas Mandal, 78–79, 84–87
semi evergreen forest, 39
Sewa Mandir, 78–84,123
Sewa Sadhana Kranti, 80
sheet rock area, 41
shifting cultivation, 41
snow-covered area, 41
stony wasteland, 41
swampy land, 40

tanks, 41
todaro, M.P., 18

Ubeshwar Vikas Mandal, activities of, 78–79, 84, 88, 100–01, 123
Udaipur: area of activity of NGOs in, 99–101; indices for, 98; NGOs activity in, 78–101; villages studied, *see*, Villages of Udaipur district studied

Villages of Udaipur district studied: access to infrastructural facilities, 109–10; cattle stock ownership pattern, 114–16; cropping pattern, 114–15; drinking water resources, 112; forest land quality utilization and upgradation, 116–17; groundwater utilization and its characteristics, 114; health, education and community infrastructure, 107–09; household level variables, 41; household participation in commons, 129–34; impact of institutional innovation, 123–26; individual/household migration, 126–28; institutional innovation and evolution, 121–26; inter village variations, 105; irrigation from seasonal streams, 112; irrigation sources ownership pattern, 113; land ownership and use pattern, 110–11; location of, 105; magnitude of participation in commons, 134–36; migrational patterns in, 117–18; natural resources management, 103–18; non-governmental initiatives in, 103–18; policy implications, 151–53; selection of villages, 104; simultaneous structural system, 136–39; socio demographic profile, 105–07; sources and ownership pattern of water resources, 111–14; summary of findings of study, 146–51; summary statistics for selected variables, 142–45; variables and methodology, 123–26

Wasteland, 31–33, 40–41; and CPR land, 31–33
Water bodies, 41.

About the Authors

KANCHAN CHOPRA is Professor and Head of the Environmental Economics Unit, Institute of Economic Growth, Delhi. She specialises in agriculture, resource and environmental economics and has authored and co-authored several books, the most recent one being *Operationalising Sustainable Development: Ecological-Economic Modelling for Developing Countries* (with G.K. Kadekodi). Professor Chopra is also associate editor of *Environment and Development Economics* (University of Cambridge), a member of the Expert Committee on Environmental Economics set up by the Ministry of Environment and Forests, Government of India, and founder President of the Indian Society for Ecological Economics.

S.C. GULATI is Professor and Head of the Population Research Center, Institute of Economic Growth, Delhi. He specialises in econometrics and population-environment studies. He has authored and co-authored several books including *Fertility in India: An Econometric Analysis of a Metropolis, Women's Status and Reproductive Health Rights, Contraceptive Use in India,* and *Socioeconomic Root Causes of Biodiversity Loss in Chilika Lake* (forthcoming). He has coordinated several research projects for the World Resource Institute, Washington, the World Wide Fund for Nature, India, the World Bank, the United Nations Population Fund and the National Commission for Women, India.